Cyber Resilience
A Global Challenge

Virginia A. Greiman
Emmanuelle Bernardin

Cyber Resilience: A Global Challenge
Virginia A. Greiman and Emmanuelle Bernardin

First edition, August 2021
Copyright © 2021 the Authors

ISBN: 978-1-914587-02-3

Published by: ACPIL, Reading, RG4 9AY, United Kingdom,
info@academic-conferences.org Available from www.academic-bookshop.com

Contents

iii

About the Authors

 **Virginia A. Greiman** is an Assistant Professor at Boston University where her teaching and research focuses on international law and cyber regulation, national cyber security strategies, and leading complex infrastructure projects. She has published over 60 scholarly articles and has served as a high-level appointee and advisor to the U.S. Department of Justice and the U.S. Department of State.

 **Dr. Emmanuelle Marie Bernardin** is Professor of Information Systems, Head of Pedagogy of the Management Department, Audencia Business School, Nantes, France. Her teaching and research focus on human-centred approaches to organizational project management, strategic information systems, and digital transformation. Her current research is on higher education digital transformation and resilience.

.

Acknowledgements

The authors would like to thank Paul Simon for his early contribution to the taxonomic development of resilience and Russ McRee for his contribution and perspectives on cyber resilience. Although this book is a work in progress, we would like to thank those who assisted in our endeavor to understand more deeply the meaning of cyber resilience as it applies across the tactical, operational, and strategic levels of an organization and how we might better manage the challenges and uncertainties of cyberspace and advance toward a safer and more resilient world.

Foreword

The rapid development of Digital Transformation has enabled profound changes in the strategies and operations across different industries around the world. Yet, this digitalisation has not only opened up new opportunities for individuals and businesses to obtain information, conduct business and communicate, but also has brought more vulnerabilities and risen the tide of threats allowing cybercriminals to conduct ever more sophisticated, targeted, and destructive cyberattacks. Every year, a new wave of cyber-attacks is affecting a significant number of organizations across a wide range of industries, and they are not showing any signs of slowing down in the near future. Several huge cyber-attacks have already made the headlines during 2021 such as:

- *Bombardier*, the Canadian plane manufacturer, suffered a data breach in February 2021. The breach resulted in the compromise of the confidential data of suppliers, customers and around 130 employees located in Costa Rica.
- *Acer*, the world 6th-largest PC vendor, was hit with a $50 million ransomware demand.
- *The University of California*, San Francisco paid a ransom of $1.14 million after the NetWalker ransomware locked down multiple servers of its School of Medicine.
- *CNA Financial*, one of the largest insurance firms in the U.S., reported a cyber-attack that disrupted the organization's customer and employee services for three days. It caused a network disruption and impacted certain CNA systems, including corporate email.
- T-Mobile Hacker Stole Data on 50 Million Customers

These examples show that absolute security is impossible. With new digital technology and innovations usages and adoption, come new risks. It is now no longer a matter of 'if' but 'when' an organization will suffer a cyber-attack, especially in our increasingly digital world. These threats and cyberattacks will keep increasing and become more creative by finding new ways to exploit the users and technology to access passwords, networks, and valuable data. They will impact the business chain value dynamics and prevent organizations from pursuing new growth opportunities, entering new markets to launching a new sales channel or delivering new and improved customer experience. Witnessing the extent of damage cyber-attacks can cause should be reason enough to take the necessary preventive measures right away. Unfortunately, when it comes to advancing their security controls, organizations still function with a vague cyber resilience strategy.

Given today's increasingly evolving threat landscape, cyber resilience has become one of the most important factors in determining the success of an organization. It has emerged over the past few years because traditional cyber security measures are no longer enough to protect organizations from the spate of persistent attacks. Adopting a cyber-resilience strategy is a priority because cyber security is about reacting while cyber resilience is about anticipating the hidden risks in the actual digital economy. It will enable organizations operating in critical environments to defend themselves from attacks that are looming in the distance, maintain business continuity, and stay competitive.

This essential book will give a clear overview of cyber resilience challenges and bring more clarity to the concept of resilience and how to develop a concrete operational strategy in all organizations including multi-national corporations, small private companies as well as regional and national governments. Featuring real-world case studies, as well as providing an interesting comparison of resilience strategies between the United States and Europe, this book is packed with clear explanations, sound advice, and practical examples to help you understand and apply the principles of cyber resilience effectively.

Redouane El Amrani,
Associate Professor
Audencia Business School, France

Chapter 1

Introduction to Cyber Resilience

As cyber threats evolve, we need to evolve as well
Christopher A. Wray, Director, FBI

Technology is at a critical moment in history. Artificial Intelligence (AI) and Machine Learning (ML) are advancing faster than society's ability to absorb and understand them; at the same time, computing systems that employ AI and ML are becoming more pervasive and complex. These new capabilities can make the world safer and more affordable, just, and environmentally sound; conversely, they introduce security challenges that could imperil public and private life (NSTC, 2020). Beyond just detection and the success/failure factor, information about cyber-attacks can help protect sources and methods and provide new insights to improve resilience over time.

In addition to the impact of the changing technology on resilience, the internet is a global network, where data originating from one country can move to another at the speed of light. Moreover, the devices that make up the infrastructure of the internet have a global supply chain. The software those devices require to operate are often created by international businesses. Policies that one country establishes may have market effects in another.

The Internet-of-Things (IoT) highlights the international nature of cybersecurity. Parts of a device may be built in one country in accordance with the standards of another where they will be marketed and sold. But, since they connect to the internet, they may become infected with malware from a third country and be used against users in a fourth country where the regulations may differ widely. All of this creates challenges at the strategic, operational, and tactical level of organizations. Though cyber security has existed for decades, "cyber resilience" are still relatively new words in the cyber lexicon. The aim of this book is to explain the main concepts, definitions, and developments in the field of cyber resilience and address the current state of the art of cyber resilience and how it is being applied by nations, governments, and industry in a cyber led world. It focuses on the question, how does cyber resilience differ from other ways of thinking about privacy, safety, and security in cyberspace? We begin this introductory chapter by looking at what cyber resilience is and what it is not from the perspective of international and national organizations, private industry, governments, practitioners, and scholars and experts in the cyber field.

1.1. Cyber Resilience: General Background and Key Concepts

Once used only in physics for shock resistance, (Merriam Webster), the term resilience is now widely used in the moral domain. In the context of accelerated global change, the concept of resilience, with its roots in ecological theory and complex adaptive systems, has emerged as the favored framework for understanding and responding to the dynamics of change. Its transfer from ecological to social contexts, however, has led to the concept being interpreted in multiple ways across numerous disciplines causing significant challenges for its practical application (Davidson, et al., 2016). Today's world complexity leads researchers and practitioners to focus on the ability of the organizations to recover from setbacks, adapt well to change, and keep going in the face of adversity. For instance, resilient infrastructures — whether they be nuclear power plants, education facilities or hospitals — must be able to prepare for, and adapt to, changing conditions. This ability enables resilient infrastructures to withstand and recover rapidly from disruptions. "*It is not just the physical structure which must withstand a blow and come back, we need resilient staff, resilient management, resilient plans, and planning*" (Manto and Lockmer, 2015, p. 199).

Following this approach, "*Cyber resilience refers to the ability to continuously deliver the intended outcome despite adverse cyber events*" (Björck et al, 2015). Cyber resilience has been defined by researchers as a key strand of national security (Harrop and Matteson, 2013, p. 149). The meaning of resilience varies widely among countries, industries, and even in the scholarly research. For example, resilience is used in many national strategies, without a clear definition but generally as the capacity of an information system or network to continue to operate despite incidents, or to carry on normal operations smoothly notwithstanding technical problems (OECD, 2019). In the scholarly research, resilience has been commonly defined as the ability of the system to withstand a major disruption within acceptable degradation parameters and to recover within an acceptable time and composite costs and risks (Haimes et al., 2009), or similarly "*as the capacity to withstand, recover from and adapt to the external shocks caused by cyber risks.*" (Dupont, 2019).

The cyber resilience literature often equates resilience with risk management. Risk management can often displace the term resilience, or it can be used to explain that resilience is achieved through risk management. Risk management is commonly defined as a process to identify, assess, allocate, control, and monitor exposures arising from operations. It assists organizations in making informed decisions to mitigate or avoid risks to achieve better outcomes, and to contrast cost with benefits of action or inaction. In the military, risk management is a function of command and a key planning consideration (DoD, JP 3-0, 2018, III-19).

1.2. Cyber Resilient Frameworks and Environmental Factors

Definitions alone provide little guidance as to expected actions, accountability, governance, and organizational response. Thus, in the past decade, frameworks have been developed to further address how these definitions should be applied at the operational level. This book explores the relationship between frameworks and the environmental factors that impact these frameworks. The cyber research emphasizes how the resilience of a system should be measured not just by its technical requirements and operational standards, but should also contain the environmental elements influencing the organizational framework including cultural factors, leadership, operant knowledge and the relationship of the participants within the cyber system, and analyzes relationships as individual actors within Actor Network Theory including the connections between both human and non-human entities (Latour, 2005).

As reflected in the Director of National Intelligence's testimony to the Senate Armed Services Committee in 2017, "*perhaps the most significant counterintelligence threat to our nation, both currently and in the future, involves the rapid development and proliferation of disruptive, advanced technologies that provide adversaries with capabilities that even just a few years ago were not considered plausible*" (Senate, 2017, p. 6). Sophisticated technical collection through a variety of means is available to more adversaries than ever before and can occur virtually anywhere and involve telephones, computers, Internet, cell phones, wired and wireless networks, as well as conversations and activities in offices, homes, vehicles, and public spaces (p. 6).

Global ransomware attacks have highlighted the need to be able to access critical IP, systems, and infrastructure even when it's locked down by ransomware. The ransomware attack on Colonial Pipeline on May 7, 2021, exemplifies the huge challenges the U.S. faces in shoring up its cyber defenses and sends a message to the world that no country is immune from these malicious actors. Colonial Pipeline, a private company, which controls a significant component of the U.S. energy infrastructure and supplies nearly half of the East Coast's liquid fuels, was vulnerable to an all-too-common type of cyber-attack. The FBI has attributed the attack to a Russian cybercrime gang emphasizing the difficulty for the government to mandate better security at private companies, and the government's inability to provide that security for the private sector (FBI, 2021). This attack was followed shortly after by a series of attacks on health care organizations worldwide including a ransomware cyberattack on Ireland's health system that paralyzed the country's health services for a week, cutting off access to patient records, delaying Covid-19 testing, and forcing cancellations of medical appointments creating a serious health crisis (NYT, 2021).

The WannaCry 2017 ransomware attack impacted multiple industries and companies worldwide, including automobile manufacturing plants that had to halt production for some time. Regardless of the motivation of the attack, clearly it resulted in unplanned downtime and recovery costs to impacted companies. Ransomware can impact any type of organization. Keeping computer systems patched and, up to date, backing up data regularly, having fully tested disaster recovery plans in place, and providing education on cyber threats (e.g., phishing and ransomware) to direct employees and contractors can help to at least reduce the extent of damage from such an incident.

The recent Solar Winds and Microsoft exchange server attacks, and the Nobelium Russian led attacks on human rights and humanitarian groups in 24 countries have hastened the urgency of the appointment of a new Senate-confirmed White House Cyber Czar under the defense authorization act who would be responsible for coordinating federal cybersecurity priorities.

1.3.   The Value of Cyber Resilience

Recent studies have shown the value of cyber resilience from an enterprise cost benefit perspective (DHS, 2018). For instance, a sophisticated cyber-attack intending to shut down a critical infrastructure enterprise could shut-down the enterprise for several weeks, rather than just several days, as is typically the case with less-sophisticated cyber-attacks. Calculating the cost of lost revenue and possible customer abandonment from several week outages compared to the cost of implementing cyber resiliency design principles and techniques, is what determines whether cyber resiliency is cost effective for the enterprise. Taking a lifecycle approach, one would assume that a critical infrastructure enterprise would be hit with a sophisticated cyber-attack at least once every 5 years and would be down for several weeks. If the loss from shutdown exceeds the cost of the preventive cyber resiliency measures, then cyber resiliency is a good investment (DHS, 2018). The IBM, Ponemon Institute Study on the Cost of a Data Breach reveals the average total cost in 2019 was $3.92 million, the average size of a data breach at 25,575 records, and the time to identify and contain a breach at 279 days. The companies studied that had an incident response team and extensive testing of their response plans saved over $1.2 million per incident (Ponemon, 2020).

In the National Institute of Standards and Technology's 2018 publication, Developing Cyber Resilient Systems, the concern for cyber resiliency focuses on aspects of trustworthiness—in particular, security and resilience—and risk from the perspective of mission assurance against determined adversaries (e.g., the advanced persistent threat) (Ross, et al., 2019). Cyber resilient systems are those systems that need security measures or safeguards to be "built in" as a foundational part of the system architecture and design. Moreover, these systems display a high level of resiliency; the systems can withstand a cyber-attack and can continue to operate even in a degraded or debilitated state, further carrying out mission-essential functions (DHS, 2018).

1.4.   Cybersecurity and Cyber Resilience: Is there a difference?

Cyber resilience is *"the measure of how well an organization can actually operate normal business during a cyberattack or data breach and how quickly it can recover from the issue"* (Conkin et al., 2017). Cybersecurity is about methods, processes and practices implemented to protect data. As cyber security has been a growing concern these past 10 years, many companies have a security plan. However, only a few have thought about the way they will handle an attack or recover from it.

Scholars have suggested that cyber resilience has a much narrower strategic vision than the more diffuse activities that fall under the generic heading of cybersecurity, and that ideally these two approaches work in tandem to create a secure organization (Conkin et al., 2017). Cyber security has been described generally as the ability to prevent or mitigate an attack, while cyber resilience is the ability to adapt and carry on after an attack.

The United States Presidential Policy Directive (PPD-21) links both cyber security and resilience to infrastructure protection recognizing that U.S. efforts shall address the security and resilience of critical infrastructure in an integrated, holistic manner to reflect this infrastructure's interconnectedness and interdependency. Organizational leadership needs to set forward-looking, outcome-oriented goals with clear accountability, and to foster planning at all levels including strategic, operational, and technological approaches. The U.S. Department of Homeland Security (DHS) has found these extant definitions linked to the following four key features: (1) **Adapt**: change in management approach or adjusting response strategies in advance to disruptive events and future threats, enabled by learning on previous disruptions; (2) **Prepare**: predict, anticipate and plan for potential threats or stressors and identify and monitor critical functions of the systems at risks (3) **Withstand**: maintain business operations without performance degradation or loss of functionalities under the hazardous conditions.; and, (4) **Recover**: rebound or restore from an adverse event to full business operations, performance, and functionalities (DHS, 2018).

Global think tanks and international organizations have also looked at the difference between resilience and cyber security and have defined resilience as the ability of systems and organizations to withstand cyber events. Resilience in this context means the preparations that an organization has made with regard to threats and vulnerabilities, the defenses that have been developed, and the resources available for mitigating a security failure after it happens (WEF, 2016). Cyber resilience differs from cyber security in that, beyond technical aspects, it also focuses on business continuity.

While there are many broader definitions of cybersecurity, there is a difference between the access control of cybersecurity and the more strategic, long-term thinking cyber resilience should evoke. Additionally, since vulnerability in one area can compromise the entire network, resilience requires a conversation focused on systems rather than individual organizations (WEF, 2016).

At the organizational level, resilience is included in some definitions and frameworks, but is notably absent in others. For example, the Department of Defense Joint Publication (2018) 3-0, Joint Operations, reflecting the current guidance for conducting joint activities across the range of military operations, does not include resilience in its "terms and definitions." Nor is the term used anywhere in the Joint Operations Publication with reference to cyber operations (DoD, JP 3.0). Instead, in protecting the Department of Defense Information Network (DODIN), JP 3-0 refers to "cybersecurity" and "cyberspace" defense measures to protect, detect, respond to, restore, and react to shield and preserve information and information systems (III-13). Ironically, cyber resilience is included in the Department of Defense national strategy and includes building a more lethal force by investing in *"cyber defense, resilience, and the continued integration of cyber capabilities into the full spectrum of military operations"* (DoD, 2018, p. 6). The DoD Department of Defense Cyber Strategy stresses that it will respond to cyber threats by *"exposing, disrupting, and degrading cyberactivity threatening U.S. interests, strengthening the cybersecurity and resilience of key potential targets, and working closely with other departments and agencies, as well as with our allies and Partners"* (DoD Cyber Strategy, 2018, p. 2).

In summary, cyber security and cyber resilience should be recognized as two distinct, but complementary disciplines. Resilience is a change from vulnerability and patch management to a longer-term strategy addressing information security gaps such as the lack of information technology products with the trustworthiness necessary to achieve information system resilience in the face of advanced persistent threats (NIST, 2018).

1.5.   Cyber Resilience and Risk Management

Resilience can provide a philosophical and methodological basis to address systemic risk in a more useful way than traditional approaches based on risk management (Linkov et al., 2019). Prevention is always a good thing, it is no longer a question anymore about "if" a company will be attacked, it is a matter of "when". However, they must have a global plan. Risk assessment and management are used to harden components of the systems affected by specific threats, yet such approaches are often prohibitively expensive to implement, and do not address cascading effects of system failure (Linkov, et al., 2019, p. 1). Risk management is a complex, multifaceted activity that generally requires the involvement of the entire organization (NIST, 2018, p. 8). The National Institute of Standards Framework describes an increasing degree of rigor and sophistication in cybersecurity risk management practices. They help determine the extent to which cybersecurity risk management is informed by business needs and is integrated into an organization's overall risk management practices. Risk management considerations include many aspects of cybersecurity, including the degree to which privacy and civil liberties considerations are integrated into an organization's management of cybersecurity risk and potential risk responses. (NIST, 2018). The Framework enables organizations – regardless of size, degree of cybersecurity risk, or cybersecurity sophistication – to apply the principles and best practices of risk management to improving [cyber] security and resilience (NIST, 2018).

As distinct from a focus on risk assessment and monitoring, resilience approaches emphasize the characteristics and capabilities that allow a system to recover from and adapt to disruption, and a commonly accepted definition describes resilience as the ability of a system to perform four functions with respect to adverse events: planning and preparation; absorption; recovery; and adaptation (Linkov, et al., 2019). While risk management and resilience approaches share some of the same concerns, there is a fundamental difference in the timeframes in which they operate. Risk is concerned with what happens before an event – preparing the system for a given threat; resilience is concerned with how the system behaves after the event occurs and how the network effects other systems. It is important to differentiate resilience from risk management, although they are intertwined (Dupont, 2019). Risk management involves quantification of the probability and severity of risks, making it possible to support decisions about the most appropriate strategy to address them, such as avoidance, acceptance, duplication, mitigation, or transfer. Resilience is broader in scope and "*is essential when risk is incomputable, such as when hazardous conditions are a complete surprise or when the risk analytic paradigm has been proven ineffective*" (Linkov et al., 2019). Resilience takes over from risk management when the latter has been ineffective at shielding an organization from disruptive threats and implies a constant cycle of activities and responses ——starting well ahead of an adverse event and concluding well after the event has ended—to implement the adaptive measures needed to counter the next unpredictable shock (Dupont, 2019). Essentially, while risk management is concerned with identifying and minimizing risk exposures before the fact, cyber-resilience seeks to maintain high performance levels irrespective of the presence or absence of an exposure (Bagheri and Ridley, 2017). Notably, cybersecurity risks that cause unexpected or unreliable behavior in a system do not always result in complete failure of an information system to fulfill its duty in support of business objectives. Many elements of a security plan are implemented to support redundancy and resilience so that a highly likely threat event might result in manageable consequences. Resilient enterprise systems may be able to continue operating in the face of adverse circumstances (Stine, et al., 2020).

1.6. Enterprise Risk Management

The increasing frequency, creativity, and severity of cybersecurity attacks means that all enterprises should ensure that cybersecurity risk is receiving appropriate attention within their enterprise risk management (ERM) programs (Stine, et al., 2020), as well as their cyber resilience risk management program. An important part of achieving risk-awareness processes is the understanding of senior leaders/executives of: (i) the types of threat sources and threat events that can adversely affect the ability of organizations to successfully execute their missions/business functions); (ii) the potential adverse impacts/consequences on organizational operations and assets, individuals, other organizations, or the Nation if the confidentiality, integrity, or availability of information or information systems used in a mission/business process is compromised; and (iii) the likely resilience to such a compromise that can be achieved with a given mission/business process definition, applying realistic expectations for the resilience of information technology (NIST, 2018). Providing greater clarity and understanding of the information technology infrastructure of organizations including the design and development of the associated information systems is a prerequisite for maximizing the resilience and wise use of these systems in the face of increasingly sophisticated threats. This type of clarity and understanding can be effectively achieved through the development and implementation of enterprise architecture (NIST, 2018).

Table 1.1 highlights the various ways that cyber security, risk management and cyber resilience is portrayed in the literature and applied in practice.

Table 1.1: *The attributes of cyber security, risk management and cyber resilience*

Attributes	Cyber Security	Risk Management	Cyber Resilience
Definition	Measures taken to ensure the safety of an organization and its stakeholders	A system to identify, assess, respond to and control risk exposures that can affect the creation or preservation of business value	The capacity to withstand shock and recover quickly from an attack that may lead to adaptation or a new equilibrium
Purpose	Prevent and reduce the risk of cyber-attacks and protect from cyber theft and espionage	Prevention and mitigation of internal and external risks both at the enterprise and individual level	Maintain high performance levels irrespective of cyber-attack exposure

Attributes	Cyber Security	Risk Management	Cyber Resilience
Technology	Designed to protect an organization and users from cybercrime and breach of privacy	Designed to identify specific threats, assess unique vulnerabilities, and implement risk reduction efforts	Designed to continue delivering services in spite of cyber-attack; relies on non-technical skills such as psychology, sociology, linguistics, languages, and geopolitics
Characteristics	Investigates, remedies, and complies with plan and procedures	Identifies, assesses, and responds to risk; often integrated with cyber security	Requires organizational agility and adaptability during and after a cyber event
Focus	The engineering and infrastructure operations	The mitigation of exposures	Outward focused; Extends beyond the global infrastructure of the Internet
Approach	Follows specified operational procedures and standards; reports on the past	Follows risk management plan or framework. Reports on potential exposures	Multidisciplinary and goal driven, uncertainty reduction approach; Reports on the future
Laws/ Regulations	Laws requiring "reasonable" cyber security are presently recognized in the U.S. and other countries; Regulations such as the (EU GDPR, 2016) protects privacy rights (see chapters 4 and 5)	Lack of laws requiring risk management compliance; may be liable under a contract or negligence theory	Lack of regulation of cyber resiliency as the concept is more ambiguous than cyber security; may be liable under a negligence theory

Given the unprecedented scale and severity of cyber-risks, cyber-resilience must extend beyond the global infrastructure of the internet, focusing instead on the individual organizations that have come to depend on it to fulfill their role. At a fundamental level, for example, there is some disagreement over the true meaning of resilience: for some, it entails the capacity of a system to withstand a shock and return to its original state, while for others it implies an evolutionary process leading to adaptation and a new state of equilibrium (Dupont, 2019). At a more practical level, cyber-resilience, rather than being understood as all encompassing, has sometimes been approached narrowly. For example, company reports, while praising its virtues, often confuse cyber-resiliency with the incident response practices and methodologies which can be more easily understood by potential customers. By the same token, the industry standards that have tried to formalize the concept of cyber-resilience are predominantly focused on its engineering aspects and rarely attach as much importance to its cognitive and social dimensions.

1.7. Summary

As shown in this chapter, cyber-resilience is thus defined less by what it is than by what it seeks to replace—an obsolete model of traditional cybersecurity unable to deal with the complex and disruptive nature of cyber-risks (Dupont, 2019). We compared cyber resilience with risk management and cyber security to show the evolution of the control of cyberspace. Without a clear understanding of the role that cyber resilience plays in adapting and recovering from a cyber-attack serious damage to person and property will continue to occur. Cyber resilience cannot complete its mission by standing alone but must be fully understood in terms of its relationship with cyber security and risk management. In Chapter 2 we explore the development of a taxonomy for cyber resilience to better assist policy makers governments, and private industry in how best to structure cyber resilience as an essential component of an organization's strategic cyberspace goals.

Chapter 2

Developing a Cyber Resilience Taxonomy: History and Background

Information is the oxygen of the modern age. It seeps through the walls topped by barbed wire; it wafts across the electrified borders.

Ronald Reagan

Our overall aim in this chapter is to bring some clarity to the concept of resilience so that it can be interpreted and articulated in ways that enhance its utility. Facilitating common understandings and goals and improving the ability to measure progress in developing resilience in the cyber world should provide the basis for the practical operationalization of the concept. One of our objectives in examining the multiple meanings of resilience is to prevent resilience becoming little more than a "*rhetorical device with little influence on actual decision-making*" (Benson and Craig, 2014, p. 780), as has happened to the concept of sustainability which was originally used in the environmental context and now has extended to multiple disciplines including psychology, sociology, and ecology.

This chapter summarizes the history and background of cyber ontologies and taxonomies generally and focuses more specifically on the characteristics of various prominent taxonomies for cyber resilience. We do so by selecting definitions of resilience in the cyber context from a diversity of organizations including governmental, intergovernmental, and private industry. Since there are hundreds if not thousands of definitions of resilience our effort here is to begin the process of showing that there is a convergence of definitions but there are also some key differences. What we hope to emphasize is that different levels of cyber intrusion can elicit different responses.

We will analyze the use of taxonomies in public and private frameworks and strategy, policy, and standards development to provide resilience as a core attribute of a system. The European Union Agency for Cybersecurity (ENISA) report on ontologies and taxonomies on resilience noted that there is no consistent taxonomy for cyber security that identifies the role of resilience (ENISA, 2011a). The ENISA document defines an ontology of resilience in order to address a behavioral dimension of the topic with a taxonomy of resilience, network, and security terms at its core. Most standard development organizations (SDOs) approach to resilience is to separate definition from use and assume terms are always understood. As noted by ENISA, in practice it can be shown that many existing standards, particularly in the security domain, tend towards ontologies in their structure (but not in their terminology) (ENISA, 2011a, p. 2).

2.1. Taxonomy v. Ontology

Taxonomy is defined by Merriam-Webster Online Dictionary as "*the study of the general principles of scientific classification.*" The word taxonomy is also used to denote the actual classification of objects, with the goal of developing a common language. The word taxonomy comes from the Greek taxis, meaning arrangement or order, and nomos, meaning law or science. For present day information management, the term taxonomy is used both in the narrow sense, to mean a hierarchical classification or categorization system, and in the broad sense, in reference to any means of organizing concepts of knowledge. The classic example of a hierarchical taxonomy is the Linnaean taxonomy (named after Carolus Linnaeus) of biological organisms, with the hierarchical top-down structure: kingdom, phylum, class, order, family, genus, and species (Linnaeus, 1735, 1758). If a taxonomy is a classification system, then how do we distinguish it from an Ontology? Researchers often refer to taxonomy as a "tree", whereas Ontology represents more of a "forest" (Medelyan, 2013).

Ontology is the term used to refer to the science and methods of developing a shared understanding of some domain of interest which may be used as a unifying framework to solve problems. In 1995, Gruber defined the notion of an ontology as an "*explicit specification of a conceptualization*" (Gruber, 1995). In 1997, Borst introduced an ontology as a "*formal specification of a shared conceptualization*" (Borst, 1997). In any case, the term is borrowed from philosophy, where Ontology is a systematic account of existence, a study of attributes that are connected because of their very nature (Spinoza, 1985). It is thought of as a broader conceptualization of a discipline that might encompass a number of taxonomies, with each taxonomy organizing a subject in a particular way.

As an example, the fields of systems engineering, artificial intelligence, and computer engineering are fields where ontologies play an important role in developing shared understandings of the requirements. In the specification of software systems, ontologies facilitate the process of identifying the requirements of the system and the understanding of the relationships among the components of the system. It also helps distributed teams of designers working in different domains to reason about what the system is designed for, rather than how the system supports this functionality. Cyber resilience planning requires not only skilled threat analysts but also advanced algorithmic tools such as machine learning and AI. Increasingly, these solutions can spot irregularities and emerging threats more quickly than human operators, and at lower costs (Abraham and Sims, 2021).

An ontology might encompass a number of taxonomies, with each taxonomy organizing a subject in a particular way. Without a shared understanding acting as a unifying framework, the problems and misapplication that arise from misunderstanding the meaning and application of cyber terms will continue to exaggerate conceptual and terminological confusion. Ontologies can also assist in standards development. However, it is not suggested that ontologies and taxonomies replace the existing approaches to developing standards, but rather that ontologies and taxonomies can be used to augment existing best practices (ENISA, 2011a). 'While a taxonomy is a way of describing information through classification, a sharing mechanism structures the way the information is encoded' (ENISA, 2011a). For example, Ontology as defined by the European Union Agency for Network and Information Security (ENISA) entails or embodies a set of concepts (e.g., entities, attributes, and processes), their definitions and their inter-relationships with respect to a given domain (ENISA, 2011a).

2.2. Cyber Resilience Taxonomic Development

Cyber resiliency taxonomies and ontologies have evolved from the early 1990s and today represent different characterization and methodologies for understanding not only security vulnerabilities, but also the relationships between threat actors, systems, and counter measures. Though commonly referred to as taxonomies, the distinction between taxonomies and ontologies is often blurred in the literature.

Starting in 1995, Bishop's research focused on categorizing security vulnerabilities in software to assist security practitioners in maintaining more secure systems through an understanding of these vulnerabilities (Bishop, 1995). John Howard built on Bishop's idea in his work in which he analyzed and classified 4300 security related incidents on the internet. Howard's work was notable because he included attackers, results, and objectives as classification of categories expanding threat taxonomies beyond the technical details of an attack to include more intangible factors such as an attacker's motivation for conducting an attack (Howard, 1997).

2.3. Attack Centric Frameworks for Resilience: Threat Taxonomies

To date, most threat taxonomies are designed as attacker centric frameworks versus analysis of the attack from the perspective of the person or entity attacked (Applegate and Stavrou, 2007). Cyber-attack behavior analysis can be roughly classified as "network centric" and "attacker centric" approaches. Compared with traditional "network centric" approach, the keys to implement "attacker centric" approach are to investigate the attacker relationship as well as tracking attackers. Killourhy, Maxion and Tan created a defense-centric based taxonomy in 2004 on how an attack manifested itself in the target systems (Killourhy et al., 2004). Supported by the Office of Naval Research, researchers at the University of Memphis created a cyber-attack taxonomy called **AVOIDIT** in 2009 which focused exclusively on cyber-attacks (Simmons, et al., 2009). AVOIDIT described attacks using five extensible classifications:

(1) Attack Vector, (2) Operational Impact, (3) Defense, (4) Informational Impact and (5) Target

This taxonomy was created as a network architecture which, unlike previous efforts, allowed the classification of blended attacks. Further, it also allowed for the classification of attacks by both operational and informational impacts and was designed to help educate defenders by looking at attacks' various impacts, vectors, or target types.

In 2014 Joshi and Singh developed a five-dimensional approach towards standardization of network and computer attack taxonomies called ADMIT. The proposed taxonomy describes the nature of the attack through the following five components: (1) Attack vector, (2) Defense, (3) Method, (4) Impact and (5) Target (Joshi and Singh, 2015). Though several of the dimensions of ADMIT are similar to the AVOIDIT taxonomy, Joshi and Singh recognized that a taxonomy should be able to adapt to changes in trends that happen over time to maintain its usability. A standard vulnerability taxonomy or categorization scheme is required for efficient and effective security assessment of software systems, tools, and services. Many issues on vulnerability classifications are open for further research, such as whether the attributes discovered by the existing classifications are enough to describe any vulnerability, how to quantify each attribute of a vulnerability in order to make a reasonable network security evaluation, and how to evaluate the damage attribute of vulnerability. In addition, developing an automatic classification scheme to handle the ever-increasing vulnerability is also a main task that requires further work in this field. But does not cover the attacker's motivation for the attack.

2.4. Cyber Conflict Taxonomy

In recent years, taxonomies have focused specifically on SCADA systems describing SCADA (Supervisory Control and Data Acquisition) architecture, vulnerabilities, attacks, and counter measures (Fovino, et al. 2010). In 2010, moving away from traditional IT threat taxonomies, Cebula & Young (2010) categorized risks into four classes: (1) actions of people, (2) systems and technology failures, (3) failed internal processes, and (4) external events. Scott and Angelos (2013) proposed a cyber conflict taxonomy in 2013. Subjects of the taxonomy were entered as either events or entities and then categorized using the categories and subcategories of actions or actors. Each of these categories was then further subdivided into increasingly specific subcategories used to describe the defining characteristics of each subject and labeled lateral linkages were used to illustrate the associative relationships between entities and events. The categories were organized in both a hierarchical and associative manner to illustrate the relationships between subjects, and categories (Joshi, et al., 2015).

2.5. The Strategic Level of Cyber Taxonomies

The development of cyber taxonomies to classify network vulnerabilities and cyber-attacks has led to a greater insight into the impacts, the mitigation, and the root causes of these attacks. However, no current taxonomy addresses the terminology in the cyber domain that impacts decision making at the more strategic level within governments, nations, and transnational organizations. A considerable amount of research has been developed to classify threats and vulnerabilities at the tactical level. These taxonomies are designed as attacker-centric frameworks which categorize attacks from the perspective of an attacker's tools, motivations, and objectives. This is due to the lack of a unified ontology at the strategic level for government and enterprise-level structures. For example, if one nation or one branch of a government interprets cyber resilience to include control systems, this will have a vastly different impact from a nation or government branch that limits cyber resilience to computer hardware and linked networks.

The existing frameworks for cyber resilience and the current methodologies used to develop these frameworks separates the definitions from the application of these definitions implying that these applications are readily understood. For the U.S. resilience is defined in the Presidential Privacy Directive (PPD-21) as "*the ability to prepare for and adapt to changing conditions and withstand and recover rapidly from disruptions.*" Moreover, the definition further provides: "*resilience includes the ability to withstand and recover from deliberate attacks, accidents, or naturally occurring threats or incidents.*" Taken literally, this definition implies that attacks are to be expected and avoidance may not be a realistic option, therefore, preparation for the attack is critical. In order to do so, both governments as well as private companies must consider the issue at the strategic, operational, and tactical levels which may or may not be tethered to: (1) strategic (policy and pre-policy) level understanding of the larger operational – capabilities environment; (2) norms and practices from the public and private sector in the provision of mission-critical ICT and other elements of national power.

However, a methodology which takes into account major factors to comprehend the whole is lacking. Knowledge is power; yet knowledge requires understanding of the strategic, technical, operational, and morphological dependencies of cyber security and critical infrastructure systems-of-systems. Yet this is not fully achievable without comprehensive and collaborative definitions of key terminology. By creating a methodology that feeds a strategic level product to intake, assess, assign, and define key terms, we then will develop a solidified qualitative architecture for an actionable ontology for use by the commons. The primary purpose of the ontology and its contained taxonomy is to assist organizations in developing their own strategies, policies, standards and laws and regulations. This book is anticipated to complement extant policy documents and stimulate discussion for revision and diffusion into emergent policy. The research will respond to the Heilmeier Catechism developed by the U.S. Defense Advanced Research Projects Agency (DARPA) (Waldrop, 2015).

2.6. Developing a Taxonomic Methodology for Cyber Resilience

This section focuses on the development of an ontological taxonomic framework that complements, yet does not replace, an organization's risk management process and cybersecurity program. The framework can serve as an important source in developing a common language for international cooperation on critical infrastructure cybersecurity. As shown in Table 2.1, there are a multitude of definitions for resiliency that can be observed in these examples drawn from private industry, international organizations, military organizations, and national governments.

Table 2.1: *Developing a taxonomy for resilience*

Organization	Context/Scope	Definition
U.S. Department of Commerce	NIST Standards (2018)	Develop and implement the appropriate activities to maintain plans for resilience and to restore any capabilities or services that were impaired due to a cyber-security event. The Framework Core consists of five elements: Functions (identify, protect, detect, respond, and recover); Categories (asset management, access control, detection processes); Subcategories (provide a set of results to support achievement of the outcomes in each category); Informative References (specific sections of standards, guidelines, and practices common among critical infrastructure sectors that illustrate a method to achieve the outcomes).

Organization	Context/Scope	Definition
Microsoft Corporation	Digitally Empowering Systems	Resilience encompasses preparation for crises and ongoing challenges, whether natural or man-made (readiness), the capability to react to an event and restore normalcy (response), and the capacity to learn from and adapt to the new status quo (reinvention).
The White House (2013)	Presidential Policy Directive PPD-21	…the ability to prepare for and adapt to changing conditions and withstand and recover rapidly from disruptions. Resilience includes the ability to withstand and recover from deliberate. attacks, accidents, or naturally occurring threats or incidents.
OECD (Linkov, 2018)	Systemic Threats	Resilience – Adaptation to disruption – planning and preparation, absorption, recovery, and adaptation
Carnegie Mellon University, 2016	CERT Resilience Management Model, Version 1.2	Public/Private operational resilience requirements refers collectively to requirements that ensure the protection of high-value assets as well as their continuity when a disruptive event has occurred. The requirements traditionally encompass security, business continuity, and IT operational requirements. These include the security objectives for information assets (confidentiality, integrity, and availability) as well as the requirements for business continuity planning and recovery and the availability and support requirements of the organization's technical infrastructure (CERT 1.2).
DoD, 2011	Space Mission	Resilience is the ability of an architecture to support the functions necessary for mission success in spite of hostile action or adverse conditions. An architecture is "more resilient" if it can provide these functions with higher probability, shorter periods of reduced capability, and across a wider range of scenarios, conditions, and threats. Resilience may leverage cross-domain or alternative government, commercial, or international capabilities. (DoD, 2011)
Office of the Under Secretary of Defense for Acquisition, Technology, and Logistics, Washington, D.C. (September 2015)	DoD Program Manager's Guidebook for Integrating the Cyber-Security Risk Management Framework (RMF) into the System Acquisition Lifecycle, Version 1.0, (September 2015):	Cyber resilience is the resilience of DoD systems to cyberattacks. Cyber is broadly used to address the components and systems that provide all digital information, including weapons/battle management systems, IT systems, hardware, processors, and software operating systems and applications, both stand-alone and embedded. Resilience is defined as the ability to provide acceptable operations despite disruption: natural or man-made, inadvertent, or deliberate.
United Nations University, 2020	Implementation of whole of society cyber resilience in their national cybersecurity strategies.	As a general concept, resilience describes the capacity of a system to respond to and recover (with increased strength) from shocks, stresses, and disasters.

Organization	Context/Scope	Definition
NIAC, 2010	Critical infrastructure or enterprise security	Infrastructure resilience is the ability to reduce the magnitude and/or duration of disruptive events. The effectiveness of a resilient infrastructure or enterprise depends upon its ability to anticipate, absorb, adapt to, and/or rapidly recover from a potentially disruptive event. (NIAC, 2010)
Bargar, 2009	Academic Research	Cyberspace resilience is much more than networks. . . It is the flexibility, adaptability, and trustworthiness among the human, the physical, and the information domain. ... Cyberspace resilience is the ability to operate through cyber conflict and recover quickly to a trusted environment.

Having a definition of cyber resilience is vital for operationalizing the concept into strategic directions, processes, procedures, and evaluation frameworks. Some fundamental elements of cyber resilience could include identification of the resilient objects and resilience goals, risk assessment, adaptive management, effective communication and coordination, development of cyber aware culture and cyber capabilities across all levels of governments and society, and incident exercises. Many larger organizations may have more than one definition of cyber resilience depending on the purpose or the use of the definition within the respective components of the organization. *"Amongst a few different perspectives on resilience offered by Microsoft, the following resonates the strongest."*

Resilience encompasses preparation for crises and ongoing challenges, whether **natural or man-made** (readiness), the capability to react to an **event** and **restore** normalcy (**response**), and the capacity to **learn** from and **adapt** to the new status quo (**reinvention**) (Nicholas and Pinter, 2017).

Microsoft's definition highlights two important aspects of resilience not mentioned in any of the other definitions – specifically, the capacity to learn from a cyber event and adapt to a new status quo which may require reinvention. It is important to note that restoring normalcy may not be possible, therefore, looking forward to a new reality is important in all resilience strategies.

Russ McRee, Senior Director, MSRC Security Operations & Incident Response at Microsoft provides an additional perspective on resilience by proposing that:

"Resilience become the modern fourth member of the CIA triad: confidentiality, integrity, and availability. In light of major security events and incidents, true CIA isn't possible without resilience. Regaining confidentiality after a data breach requires resilience. Ensuring data integrity after a major storage failure demands resilience. Building services that remain available under the worst of DDoS conditions defines resilience as a core tenet. In short: embed resilience or risk failure" (R. McRee, personal communication, June 17, 2021)

In Table 2.1 the definitions show various commonalities. Each expresses a common theme of addressing situations or conditions in which disruption, adversity, errors, faults, or failures occur (Solutions, 2017), and each has consistent resiliency goals when encountering situations or conditions causing disruption, adversity, and faults including recover, withstand (i.e., maintain or resist), adapt (i.e., evolve), and anticipate (i.e., prepare). It should be noted that all ten of these definitions are accurate and appropriate for the respective organization's goals and operational requirements. It is also the case that these definitions were vetted by numerous groups and experts to refine the statements down to the most salient points possible. However, all ten definitions of resiliency are clearly different, both in scope, perspective, and thoroughness. In observing the overlaps between the definitions, the NIST and CERT definitions are most similar; they share seven key words (plan, resilience, security, event, protect, recover, and infrastructure) which is the highest level of intersection between any of the definitions. It must also be pointed out that the DoD, the White House, and Microsoft definitions share three words: "resilience" and the notable phrase "natural or man-made". Even more notable is that the only word that appears in all ten definitions is "resilience", the word that we are attempting to define. However, digging a little deeper, the NIST, DoD, and CERT definitions do share "operations" or, in the case of NIST, "functions", which is a close analog to "operations", and they all share "infrastructure" or, in the case of DoD, "components and systems". This indicates, that despite the initial observation that there are few intersections between these ten definitions, a clearer picture becomes available.

It also becomes very clear what the underlying motivation of each organization may be based on what words are in their definition, and what words are not in their definition. For example, "preparation," "response", and "restoration" is not in the DoD definition, whereas it is present in the Microsoft definition. Conversely, "operations" and the concept of "both stand-alone and embedded [systems]" are specifically listed in the DoD definition, while not present in the Microsoft definition. This speaks directly to the nature of Microsoft's business model – that of preparing for and protecting against intrusion – whereas the DoD model assumes that systems, be it hardware, software, or embedded firmware, will be in contested space and as such should be able to maintain normal operations.

2.7. Summary

Taken all together, a clear and coherent definition can be derived exclusively from the intersection of terms, thus providing what could be considered the most plausible, generally accepted definition for the term resiliency. Using natural language parsing, similar to the tools that various search engines use, will most assuredly speed up the analysis process, and will provide the graphical display that allows for quick understanding of what terms intersect. The primary goal for this exercise is to create at best a carefully crafted, or at worst a generally accepted, framework methodology for defining what resiliency is within the context of cyberspace without the direct input of the myriad governments, non-government organizations, and corporations who have already proffered their disparate definitions. This framework methodology can then be applied to other more complex and vexing terms. A generally accepted definition can serve to be the foundational element for organizations that have yet to develop their own definition, and by extension, response plans for eventual cyber-attack. It can also serve to highlight the possible omissions to management, or the organizational biases to the rest of the public.

Chapter 3

Levels of Engagement in Cyberspace: Cyber Strategic, Operational and Tactical Structures for Resilience

Two things about the NSA stunned me right off the bat: how technologically so-phisticated it was compared with the CIA, and how much less vigilant it was about security in its every iteration, from the compartmentalization of infor-mation to data encryption.

Edward Snowden

When one considers the decision-making and planning necessary to conduct mali-cious cyber activity, it becomes easier to understand how it is not simply an "on-the-network" fight. There is no broadly accepted delineation of the various levels of cyber activities commonly described in the literature as: strategic, operational, and tactical but as shown in Figure 3.1 there are common activities across organi-zations that occur at each level in the cyber realm. In this chapter we explore the current structures in place at each level and how these structures can interact to provide a more resilient engagement.

Figure 3.1: *Cyber resilience structure: Strategic, operational, tactical*

3.1. Levels of Engagement

The military approach to cyberspace provides a model for engagement. Three lev-els of warfare—strategic, operational, and tactical—model the relationship be-tween national objectives and tactical actions. The operational level of warfare links the tactical employment of forces to national strategic objectives (DoD, JP 3-

0, 2018, p. xi). The level of complexity, duration, and resources depends on the circumstances. The investment strategy is a change from vulnerability and patch management to a longer-term strategy addressing information security gaps such as the lack of information technology products with the trustworthiness necessary to achieve information system resilience in the face of advanced persistent threats (APT) (NIST, 2018).

By comparison, nations are also establishing strategies for cyberspace at various levels to address similar goals. For example, Spain conducts risk analysis at three different levels: The strategic-political level, the operational level, and the tactical-technical level. These levels act in a coordinated manner to obtain an overview of cybersecurity risks (ENISA, 2016a, p. 16). The National Security Strategy is the framework of the National Security Policy, and it contains the analysis of the strategic environment, particular risks, and threats to the security of Spain. Therefore, it is the first step in risk analysis. In addition, the National Cyber Security Council of Spain (part of the National Security Council) assesses risks and threats, analyses possible scenarios of crisis, studies its possible evolution, and develops and updates response plans. Analysis at the operational level includes the situation monitoring by various bodies and agencies with cybersecurity skills, such as the National Intelligence Centre (CNI), Joint Operation Command of the Armed Forces of Spain, or the Secretary of State for Security from the Ministry of Interior. The tactical level includes monitoring the situation by various bodies and agencies responsible for cybersecurity at the technical level. Relevant authorities on this level are the Spanish Joint Cyber Defense Command with a specialized Computer Emergency Response Team (CERT), the National Centre for Critical Infrastructure Protection (CNPIC), the Spanish National Institute of Cybersecurity (INCIBE) and the National Cryptologic Centre (ENISA, 2016a).

3.2. Strategic Level Engagement

Resilience will succeed only if there is a clear governance structure in place at the strategic, operational, and tactical level of an organization. A governance framework defines the roles, responsibilities, and accountability of all relevant stakeholders. It provides a framework for dialogue and coordination of various activities undertaken in the lifecycle of the strategy.

Strategic engagement often occurs at the level at which a nation, often as a member of a group of nations, determines national or multinational (alliance or coalition) strategic security objectives and guidance, then develops and uses national resources to achieve those objectives (DoD, JP 3-0, 2018). Though associated with the Department of Defense (DoD), strategic cyber requirements apply equally to the private sector. It is a high-level responsibility to orient strategic cyber analysis resources against the enterprise's most critical mission and business needs and strategy, rather than leaving it to the lower-level cyber security analysts. An overall enterprise approach taking into account risk versus benefit needs to be applied (INSA, 2015). Strategic level engagement exists in every organization, across every industry, and encompasses concepts, visions, mission statements, policies, and laws and regulations.

A strategic plan is ultimately a statement of how an organization will use its finite resources to accomplish its mission. In some organizations it can be viewed as a sustainability document. In the context of cyber resilience, organizations may think of sustainability in different ways. While some may think of it at the economic level, others may think of it in terms of the institutional, technical, scientific, social, security and political levels. There is, then, a real question of ensuring not only sustainability of current operations and mechanisms, but also progress in terms of creating more innovative working methods, tools, and processes at the tactical level (Christou, 2016). Essential to the success of a cyber strategy is the development of a culture characterized by both continuous learning and data-driven decision-making.

3.3.   National Level Strategic Direction

As an example, the United States' Defense Department National strategic direction is governed by the Constitution, federal law, USG policy, internationally recognized law, and the national interest as represented by national security policy (DoD, JP 3-0, 2017, p. I-5). Strategic direction is typically published in key documents, generally referred to as strategic guidance, but it may be communicated through any means available and it "*may change rapidly in response to changes in the global environment, whereas strategic guidance documents are typically updated cyclically and may not reflect the most current strategic direction*" (DoD, JP 3-0, 2018, pp. I-5). For example, in its 2020 Strategic Cyber Operations Guide, the U.S. Army War College emphasizes the assessment of risk across six key areas: "*national security, energy and power, banking and finance, health and safety, communications, and transportation*" to improve the security and resilience of critical infrastructure (DoD, 2020, p. 4).

Strategies must always be connected at all levels of the organization. For example, It is a serious and sometimes grave omission when strategies are not properly incorporated into policies and procedures showing a disconnect between the strategic and the operational and tactical levels of governance. DoD also notes the difficulty of building cyber resilience strategies outside of its domain. "*In order for resilience to succeed as a factor in effective deterrence, other agencies of the government must work with critical infrastructure owners and operators and the private sector more broadly to develop resilient and redundant systems that can withstand a potential attack. Effective resilience measures can help convince potential adversaries of the futility of commencing cyberattacks on U.S. networks and systems*" (DoD, 2016).

3.4.   National Cyber Security Strategies

At the national level, strategic direction for cyber resilience can also be found in national cyber security strategies (NCSS). Presently, there are approximately 82 nations that have developed national cyber security strategies (NCSS) that are publicly available and represent both the developed and developing worlds including Afghanistan, Bangladesh, Kenya, Serbia, and Egypt (ITU, 2020). Some national strategies that are not formally published can be found in white papers and other government documents. Turkey's strategic cyber measures include regulatory changes, judicial process improvements, and a 2020-2023 National Cybersecurity Strategy and Action Plan embracing a proactive cybersecurity approach that includes 40 actions and 75 implementation steps in relation to strategic objectives including a focus on incorporating information security culture in all of Turkey's institutions and organizations (Turkey, 2020).

Contrasting the cybersecurity strategies of 10 countries reveals the following common goals, all of which are important goals every strategy should include: (1) developing cyber defense policies and capabilities; (2) achieving cyber resilience; (3) reducing cybercrime; (4) supporting industry on cybersecurity; (5) securing critical in-formation infrastructures; (6) developing the industrial and technological resources for cybersecurity; and (7) contributing to the establishment of an international cyberspace policy (Greiman, 2015). The OECD finds many of these common to all cybersecurity strategies (Organization for Economic Cooperation and Development (OECD, 2014). Table 3.1 shows the national strategies of 15 countries in the Asian Pacific, Africa, Europe, and the Middle East that have incorporated cyber resilience as a component of their national cyber security strategy. Though many countries use the term resilience in their strategy, few discuss how resilience is implemented and operationalized at a national, transnational, or regional level. The United Nations University conducted a survey of the national cyber strategies of 14 countries in the China, Asian Pacific region and found that cyber resilience is increasingly being recognized and understood as a multi-faceted (i.e., beyond the technical dimension) whole-of-society (i.e., multi-stakeholders and systemic) posture that enables countries and the global community to persist in their societal functioning in the face of imminent cyber threats (Thinyane and Christine, 2020).

Table 3.1: *Cyber resilience in national cyber strategies*

Country	National Cyber Strategy: References to Cyber Resilience
Austria	focus is on resilience for critical infrastructure by requiring that these strategic enterprises set up comprehensive security architecture (Austria, 2013).
Estonia	...in addition to preventing incidents, the focus must also be on cyber resilience; that is, the control and reduction of damage caused by incidents (Estonia, National Cyber Security in Practice (ENCP), 2020).
Germany	cyber resilience" describes an entity's ability to withstand attacks on the security of its information and communications technology (ICT). Hackers focus on an entity's systems or even customer data (BaFin, 2020, Cyber Security).
India	Resilience (involves) rapid identification, information exchange, investigation, and coordinated response, and remediation for mitigating the damage caused by malicious cyberspace activity (National Cyber Security Strategy 2020)
Ireland	To identify and protect critical national infrastructure by increasing its resilience to cyber-attack and by ensuring that operators of essential services have appropriate incident response plans in place to reduce and manage any disruption to services (Gov't of Ireland, National Cyber Security Strategy, 2019-2024).
Israel	Resilience is the systemic capacity to handle threats when they inevitably materialize (Israel, 2020).

Country	National Cyber Strategy: References to Cyber Resilience
Japan	[Resilience] (involves) adoption of a 'mission assurance' approach to reducing risks to an acceptable level and ensure the safe and continuous operations and services (Cyber Security Strategy 2018)
Mauritius	National cyber resilience will be tailored to ensure the preparedness and pre-dictive capabilities required by the goals and to facilitate its operating capabil-ity during cyber conflicts and post-conflict recovery (The Republic of Mauri-tius National Cyber Security Strategy 2014-2019).
Netherlands	The capabilities of the intelligence and security services, DefCERT and the NCSC to gain insight into threats and digital attacks, to detect them, disrupt them and increase resilience will be improved structurally (The Netherlands, (2018) National Cyber Security Agenda, Ministry of Justice and Security).
New Zealand	Resilience (involves) resistance against, and protection from cyber threats, and the ability to respond to incidents across systems (New Zealand's Cyber Security Strategy, 2019).
Philippines	The objective (of the Resilient Enterprise State) is predictive and mission-fo-cused to isolate and contain damage, secure supply chains, and protect critical infrastructure to continue operation through cyber-attacks with a focus on iden-tify, protect, detect, respond, and recover (Philippines Cyber Security Strategy and National Cybersecurity Plan 2022)
Scotland	There needs to be a whole-of-government approach to cyber resilience (Cyber Resilience Strategy for Scotland, 2015-2020).
Singapore	Cyber resilience is the ability of the critical information infrastructures to with-stand cyber-attacks, allowing them to continue operating under the toughest conditions and recover quickly after a disruption (Singapore Cyber Security Strategy 2016).
South Korea	Strengthen security and resilience of the national core infrastructure against cyber-attacks to ensure continuous provision of critical services (Republic of Korea National Cyber Security Strategy)
Sri Lanka	Resilience (includes) detection, prevention, response, and recovery capabili-ties (Information and Cyber Security Strategy of Sri Lanka (2019-2023)

Policymakers and other stakeholders alike have an interest in measuring the impact of the national cyber security strategies. This measurement can focus on both pol-icy effectiveness - i.e., to what extent security and resilience has been improved by the implementation of the NCSS and how this has affected the citizens (captured by the outcomes and impact section of the logic model); and the efficacy of the process, i.e., the extent to which the observed changes can be attributed to the spe-cific elements of the strategy (ENISA, 2013). According to the Defense Science Board (DSB, 2017) as offensive cyber capabilities continue to grow, and are likely to outpace cyber defense and resilience, there are likely to be growing risks of mis-perception that could lead to rapid cyber escalation – and the potential for rapid es-calation to armed conflict. Because benefits of offensive cyber are large and grow-ing, arms control verification is impossible, and attribution is challenging. How-ever, conducting detailed planning and wargaming can help identify ways to re-duce such risks, for example by defining key military systems for protection, establishing norms or "rules of the road," and continuing and expanding bilateral discussions of the future of strategic stability (DSB, 2017). *"The U.S. Government must work with the private sector to intensify efforts to defend and boost the cyber resilience of U.S. critical infrastructure in order to avoid allowing extensive vulnerability to these nations. It is no more palatable to allow the United States to be held hostage to catastrophic attack via cyber weapons by such actors than via nuclear weapons"* (DSB, 2017).

3.5. Operational Resilience: Strategic Leadership

If an organization intends to be operationally resilient this requires senior level involvement. According to the Intelligence and National Security Alliance (INSA), the involvement of senior leadership is critical for a strategic cyber intelligence program to be an effective component of risk management. Senior leaders are the consumers, and it is their role to define and clearly communicate the organization's critical intelligence requirements (INSA, 2014).

NIST also emphasizes this point:

To be effective, organization-wide risk management programs require the strong commitment, direct involvement, and ongoing support from senior leaders. The objective is to establish, strategic risk assessment and then institutionalize the appropriate risk management into the day-to-day operations of an organization as a priority and an integral part of how organizations conduct operations in cyberspace (NIST, 2018).

There are clear benefits to be gained from implementing intelligence-led cyber resilience, not just in terms of proactively managing an array of new and evolving advanced cyber threats but also the potential for improving risk management and high-level business strategy. The Bank of England provides an intelligence led view of cyber resilience by moving beyond the technical details of the attack (the what, when, and where) towards a better understanding, and attribution, of the tactics, techniques, and procedures (TTPs) behind the attack (the modus operandi or how) and, critically, the attackers themselves (the who and why). Such intelligence places cyber threats in context and, through greater situational awareness, better informs the countermeasures. In this way, through better understanding, information security can move from reactive, 'seize and wipe' defense to responsive, proactive, intelligence-led cyber resilience (BoE, 2016, p. 3).

3.6. Operational Level Engagement

Within the U.S. military, the operational level engagement is the level at which campaigns and major operations are planned, conducted, and sustained to achieve strategic objectives within theaters or other operational areas (DoD, JP 3-0, 2018). The focus at this level is on planning and execution of operations. Operations may include planning where, when, how and for what purpose military forces will be employed, to influence the adversary's disposition before combat, to deter adversaries from supporting enemy activities, and to assure our multinational partners to achieve operational and strategic objectives (JP 3-0, 2018, I-14). This level is largely managed at the government level by agencies, departments and sub-departments of federal, state, and local government including Homeland Security, U.S. Naval Operations, and the U.S. Department of Commerce, and within the private sector at the CIO or CISO levels to understand what is happening within the network infrastructure or the cloud infrastructure.

Carnegie Mellon University published the CERT Operational Resilience Management Model in 2016 and referred collectively to "*operational resilience requirements*" as those that ensure the protection of high-value assets as well as their continuity when a disruptive event has occurred (Carnegie, 2016).

The operational environment is the composite of the conditions, circumstances, and influences that affect the employment of capabilities and bear on the decisions of the commander. It encompasses physical areas and factors of the air, land, maritime, and space domains and the information environment (which includes cyberspace). Understanding the operational environment helps the commander to better identify the problem; anticipate potential outcomes; and understand the results of various friendly, adversary, and neutral actions and how these actions affect achieving the military end state (DoD, JP 5.0, xx-xxi).

Some examples of operational level engagement are found in the Intelligence and National Security Alliance (INSA) Operational Report: (1) trend analysis indicating the technical direction in which an adversaries capabilities are evolving; (2) Indications that an adversary has selected an avenue of approach for targeting your organization; (3) Indications that an adversary is building capability to exploit a particular avenue of approach; (4) The revelation of adversary tactics, techniques, and procedures and understanding the technical, social, legal, financial, or other vulnerabilities that the adversary has; and (5) Understanding of the adversary operational cycle (i.e. decision making, acquisitions, command and control methods for both the technology and the personnel). Information that enables the defender to influence an adversary as they move through the kill chain (INSA, 2013, p. 9). The operational level links the tactical employment of forces to national strategic objectives (DoD, JP 3-0, 2018, p. I-5).

3.7. Resilience Management Operational Stages

Figure 3.2 highlights the stages of resilience with respect to time and space. Adopted in part from the OECD's (2019) model of Resilience in Systems, it emphasizes the important stages in combating disruptions (Linkov, et al., 2019). The preparation phase represents not only the first stage in resilience but also the tactics that are utilized for cyber security and risk management at an earlier phase. However, various operational and tactical elements may overlap when moving from cyber security as a preventive process to cyber resilience once an attack has occurred. A central requirement for analysis is to frame resilience as a function of both time and space due to the multi-temporal and cross-disciplinary view by which one must review systemic threats (Linkov, et al., 2019, p. 11). By operationalizing resilience, we gain an understanding of the evolution of an attack from one subsystem to another and the enormity of the impact on an entire eco system.

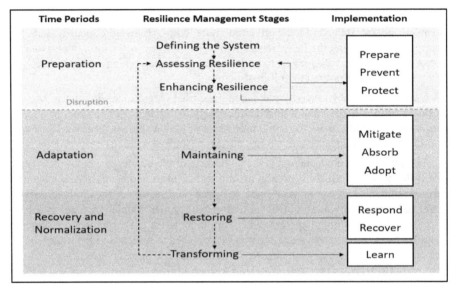

Figure 3.2: *Resilience management operational stages.* Adopted in part from OECD's 2019 Model of Resilience in Systems

3.8. Disaster Resilience and Disaster Risk Reduction

The disaster relief literature provides a wealth of knowledge on disaster management that is remarkably similar in context to the goals of cyber resilience and contains the same stages as shown in Figure 3.2. The National Academy of Sciences 2012 report on disaster resilience notes if a system is viewed in its entirety one can better understand how to plan, prepare for, absorb, recover from, and adapt to a new normal after disruptions and threats (NAS, 2012).   Disaster resilience has been defined by the United Nations Disaster Relief Reduction Organization (UNISDR) as the ability of individuals, communities, organizations, and states to adapt to and recover from hazards, shocks, or stresses without compromising long-term prospects for development. According to the Hyogo Framework for Action (UNISDR, 2016), disaster resilience is determined by the degree to which individuals, communities and public and private organizations are capable of organizing themselves to learn from past disasters and reduce their risks to future ones, at international, regional, national, and local levels. Disasters are exacting a huge toll with hundreds of thousands of lives and US$1.5 trillion lost in the last decade alone. Economic losses from disasters are now averaging US$250 billion to $300 billion each year (UNISDR, 2015). This trend is set to continue as exposure in hazard-prone countries grows more rapidly than vulnerability is reduced (UNISDR, 2015).

As described in the strategic disaster resilience framework of the UNISDR, *"the progress that countries make in these areas will be measured against the seven global targets: substantially reducing: (a) the loss of lives, (b) numbers of affected people, (c) economic loss, and (d) damage to critical infrastructure; and increasing and improving: (e) national and local strategies with specific targets and indicators, (f) international cooperation, and (g) access to early warning and risk assessment.*" Furthermore, major changes in attitudes and behaviors towards disaster risk reduction, which began in the aftermath of the Indian Ocean Tsunami of 2004, are now reflected and further elaborated in all the recent international agreements (SAMOA Pathway, Sendai Framework for Disaster Risk Reduction 2015-2030, Addis Ababa Action Agenda on financing for development, the Transforming our World: 2030 Agenda for Sustainable Development, the Paris Agreement on climate change and the New Urban Agenda). In the United Nations Sustainable Development Goals (SDGs) in particular, disaster risk reduction and resilience are reflected in 25 targets and in 10 of the 17 goals (UNISDR, 2016).

3.9.   Tactical Level Engagement

In the military, tactics is the employment, ordered arrangement, and directed actions of forces in relation to each other. Joint doctrine focuses this term on planning and executing battles, engagements, and activities at the tactical level to achieve military objectives assigned to tactical units or task forces (TFs) (DoD, JP 3-0, 2018, I-14). Malicious actors can range from a nation-state stealing government secrets, to a business competitor trying to gain a market advantage, to ideologically motivated hacktivists. Regardless, each step along the way presents an opportunity to thwart attacks (INSA, 2013). The U.S. Department of Defense, Joint Publication 1-02 defines the tactical level as: "*The level ... at which battles, and engagements are planned and executed to achieve military objectives assigned to tactical units or task forces. Activities at this level focus on the ordered arrangement and maneuver of combat elements in relation to each other and to the enemy to achieve combat objectives*" [emphasis added]. The tactical level of the cyber domain is where the on-the-network actions take place. This is where malicious actors and network defenders maneuver against each other. This is where botnets are directed towards a specific target and then unleash their payload. This is where an adversary finds a vulnerability and infiltrates a network (INSA, 2013).

3.9.1.   Private Sector Tactical Engagement

The private sector has filled many of the gaps present at the tactical level to support or more often to implement new actions to enhance cyber resilience that may not be possible within governments or transnational organizations. Cyber tactics are often used to describe various actions that are recommended to protect, detect, and respond to attacks. Microsoft's Cyber Defense Operations Center (CDOC) teams employ automated software, machine learning, behavioral analysis, and forensic techniques to create an intelligent security graph of its environment. For, example Microsoft's detect tactics include monitoring network and physical environments 24x7x365 for potential cybersecurity events, and behavior profiling, based on usage patterns and an understanding of unique threats to their services (Microsoft Secure Blog, 2017). Identity and behavioral analytics are developed to highlight abnormal activity. Machine learning software tools and techniques are routinely used to discover and flag irregularities. Advanced analytical tools and processes are deployed to further identify anomalous activity and innovative correlation capabilities. Microsoft's respond tactics include Automated response systems using risk-based algorithms to flag events requiring human intervention. Well-defined, documented, and scalable incident response processes within a continuous improvement model helps to keep Microsoft ahead of adversaries by making these available to all responders. Subject matter expertise work across Microsoft teams, in multiple security areas, including crisis management, forensics, and intrusion analysis. A deep understanding of the platforms, services and applications operating in cloud datacenters provides a diverse skill set for addressing incidents. Wide enterprise searching across both cloud, hybrid and on-premises data and systems to determine the scope of the incident. Deep forensic analysis, for major threats, are performed by specialists to understand incidents and to aid in their containment and eradication. Microsoft's security software tools, automation and hyper-scale cloud infrastructure enable Microsoft's security experts to reduce the time to detect, investigate, analyze, respond, and recover from cyberattacks (Microsoft Strategy Brief, 2017).

3.10. Summary

This chapter emphasizes that clear governance is required for cyber resilience at the tactical, operational, and strategic levels of an organization and that the strategic plan is essential in accomplishing the mission. This demands an offensive all hands-on-deck 24x7x365 approach to monitoring the network and physical environments for potential attacks in whatever form they surface. We should look for guidance to models both within and outside the cyber realm including the successful disaster management planning that has successfully reduced the potential for extensive, long-term catastrophic loss. Though increasingly countries are incorporating resilience in their national cyber strategies, there is a need to take it to the next step and implement and operationalize resilience at the national, transnational, and regional levels.

Chapter 4

The Global Context of Cyber Resilience

It is my belief that industry and government around the world should work even more closely to protect the privacy and security of Internet users, and promote the exchange of ideas, while respecting legitimate government considerations.

Bill Gates

This chapter surveys the meaning of cyber resiliency from the perspectives of national, regional, and transnational organizations as defined by governing entities. The overlap among each of these dimensions will also be discussed. For example, NATO is defined by some as both a regional and transnational organization requiring allegiance to both roles that may lead to conflicts. The chapter explores the various mechanisms used to develop resilient systems and the critical impacts arising from the power struggles that may occur between these competing dimensions. From a policy-making perspective, there is no global definition of cyber-resilience, and therefore only limited agreement on how to achieve it. Policy development at the global level will be difficult until there is a consensus on the meaning of resilience.

As noted in the OECD G-20 Report on Digital Transformation, digitalization is changing the world faster than many laws have evolved. Designing and implementing a whole-of-government approach to digitalization is crucial in this regard because advances in one area can be mitigated by retaining the status quo in another (OECD, 2017, p. 10). Also recognizing digitalization's effect on competition, and the need for looking at data as the most vital competitive asset in some markets, requiring different approaches to market definition and market power, and a greater focus on international cooperation and coordination among competition authorities (p. 10).

With the May 2017 "WannaCry" attacks targeting 74 countries across Europe and Asia demanding the payment of ransom and impacting the public health in Great Britain, the 2016 and 2017 attacks on the American and European political systems, and the 2017 attacks on the cyber systems operated by the Ukrainian government, it is clear that the negative impacts from interdependent system degradations are becoming more ominous. At the transnational level, the European Union Agency for Network and Information Security (ENISA) identified several key principles that should be considered during the development and implementation of a program designed to measure cyber resilience (ENISA, 2011b). Good metrics should be quantifiable, repeatable, and comparable to allow for viable and accurate comparison of different measurements. Good metrics should also possess some non-technical business characteristics that support the organizations business values and strategic mission. As described in later chapters, the European Union plays an important role in setting and discussing norms and debating resilience measures to support member states. However, in terms of technical, operational, and political harmonized measures, there are still significant differences between individual member states and the EU.

4.1.   The Global Landscape of Resilience

The landscape of global cyber resilience must be understood from various dimensions including strategies, policies, standards, procedures, laws, and regulations. Cyber resilience has been addressed differently by the United States and other nations. In this chapter an analysis of how countries aim to achieve cyber resilience through (1) legislation; (2) national competent authorities; (3) international trade agreements and (4) national and international standards and norms is discussed.
As an example, the functioning of the Estonian state and society, the economic and social well-being of every person, their life and health, increasingly depend on the security of the systems and services. One of the main aims of the strategy is to describe methods for ensuring the uninterrupted operation and resilience of vital services, and the protection of critical information infrastructures against cyber threats (Kohler, 2020). A major objective is to ensure that Estonia is a sustainable digital society with strong technological resilience and readiness to cope with crises. This includes, amongst other things, adherence to information security and data protection principles, broad-based implementation of the Estonian ISKE baseline security requirements, and the systematic assessment and administration of risks related to next generation technologies in fields such as cryptography, blockchain technology, artificial intelligence (AI), and secure identity management (Kohler, 2020).

In 2013, a White Paper was published in France in response to the assessment that cyber-attacks against the network and information systems of numerous French businesses and public sector enterprises were increasing in number and sophistication. This created a major paradigm shift in France from a focus on its own cybersecurity requirements to include operators whose "*unavailability could strongly threaten the ... security or resilience of the nation*" (CIIP, 2013). Japan has also stepped up its resilience requirements by the continuous collection of data in actual environments and improving defense capabilities, by incorporating cybersecurity into the planning phase of the R&D projects promoted by the Government (Japan, 2015). Some countries, like Austria, do not refer to resilience generally, but rather focus on resilience for critical infrastructure by requiring that these strategic enterprises set up comprehensive security architecture (Austria, 2013). Other countries like Israel have developed a dedicated centralized cyber security authority that comprises the intelligence community, law enforcement, international partners, and commercial partners (Israel, 2020). Israel's strategy consists of a robust, resilient, and defense-based approach to cyber security that addresses the capacity to disrupt cyber-attacks by focusing on the human factors behind them. Resilience is defined in the strategy as the systemic capacity to handle threats when they inevitably materialize (Housen-Couriel, 2017). In Saudi Arabia, the focus is on building a resilient supply chain. At the Saudi Arabia Cyber World Summit in 2020 in a keynote on Cyber Security Technologies for Smart Cities of the Future, Mike Loginov, CISO & CTO of NEOM, Saudi Arabia, remarked: "*The next evolution is the advent of the cognitive city. NEOM will be built on IoT devices, so the first criterion is to push the onus out on to the supply chain. We want to know that the technologies are properly tested before we deploy them in the live environment. We have to ensure every one of those is secured to the highest level.*" Australia in its new 2020 cyber security strategy provides an enhanced framework intended to uplift security and resilience in critical infrastructure sectors, combined with better identification and sharing of information about threats in order to make Australia's critical infrastructure – whether owned or operated by industry or government – more resilient and secure (Australia, 2020).

4.2. National Cyber Strategies

As described by ENISA (2014) the main points covered by a typical National Cyber Security Strategy are: (1) To define a governance framework for cyber security. (2) To define an appropriate mechanism (often a public private partnership) that allows all relevant public and private stakeholders to discuss and agree on different policy and regulatory cyber security issues. (3) To outline and define necessary policy and regulatory measures and clearly defined roles, responsibilities, and rights of the private and public sector (e.g., new legal framework for fighting cybercrime, mandatory reporting of incidents, minimum security measures and guidelines, and new procurement rules). For example, the strategy from Slovakia identifies a need to define a legal framework for the protection of cyberspace (Slovak Republic, 2015). To set the goals and means to develop national capabilities and the necessary legal framework to engage in the international efforts of diminishing the effects of cybercrime. In several strategies there is a particular focus on cybercrime. The Lithuanian (2018) strategy states that Lithuania "*is eager to become an active partner in the international community which seeks to resolve cyber security and internet governance problems.*" Lithuania is active in building cooperation with partners and allies including the United States by signing an international agreement for legal regulation of cyberspace which shall comply with the provisions of international law, standards and principles that apply to activities in cyberspace in relation to protection of the open Internet principle as well as other principles on fundamental freedoms and human rights. This may also mean an integration of existing structures (e.g., national/governmental CERTs).

According to a study conducted by The Hague Center for Strategic Studies for the European Economic and Social Committee (EESC) corporate Europe faces a wide range of challenges in identifying, preparing for, and responding to cyber threats and incidents. Lack of a system to share information stands out as the number one inhibitor, both from an external, public policy perspective, and from the internal, company perspective. This concerns information sharing between individual member States, between governments and private enterprises, between CSIRTs, and between individual enterprises across industries and borders (EESC, 2018).

4.3. National Strategy Implementation

In earlier chapters we looked at the definitions of cyber resilience and in this chapter, we explore models for resilience. A review of National Strategies for Resilience highlights those countries that have advanced beyond traditional cyber security models and are thinking about models for resilience that go beyond protect and defend and have moved into the real heart of a resilience strategy which is to be able to survive an attack, recover from an attack, learn from an attack, and reinvent a new way of operating after a cyber-attack that provides stability for the longer-term future (Nicholas and Pinter, 2017).

We can look to Europe for some frameworks specifically in Denmark, Germany, and the UK. According to the 2020 United Nation (UN) e-government survey, Denmark is now the World's best in e-government initiatives, followed by the Republic of Korea, Estonia, Finland, Australia, Sweden, the United Kingdom of Great Britain and Northern Ireland, New Zealand, the United States of America, the Netherlands, Singapore, Iceland, Norway, and Japan.

Among the world's least developed countries, Bhutan, Bangladesh, and Cambodia have become leaders in digital government development, advancing from the middle to the high E-Government Development Index (EGDI) group in 2020. Mauritius, the Seychelles, and South Africa are leading the e-government ranking in Africa. Overall, 65 per cent of Member States are at the high or very high EGDI level (UN, 2021).

Denmark is ranked first among the 193 United Nations Member States based on its scope and quality of online services, status of telecommunication infrastructure and existing human capacity according to the assessment by the UN Department of Economic and Social Affairs (UNDESA). Among Denmark's initiatives in the digital space is the *"Government's GovTech program to help tech startups deliver,"* fostering safe spaces for innovation and experimentation (UN, 2021).

Developing new solutions to create public sector value, Denmark has for the last 18 years quite aggressively followed an ambitious digital agenda for its public sector. Importantly, Denmark takes a broader approach to cyber resilience that encompasses cyber security and business continuity management and aims to defend against potential cyber-attacks and ensure an organization's survival following an attack. As described in the Danish Government's Cyber and Information Security Strategy 2018-2021, six sectors are particularly vulnerable in the event of a cyberattack in Denmark. These sectors are the energy sector, the transport sector, the telecommunications sector, the financial sector, the healthcare sector, and the maritime sector. In the event of a cyberattack against a power plant, for example, large parts of Denmark will break down. This will have consequences for much of society (Denmark, 2018).

A recent study on "Digital Organizational Resilience" in Denmark found three elements – new ways of strategizing, cross-sectoral collaboration, and new ways of learning – occurred with regularity throughout the history of Denmark's digitization process, *"and constitute a pattern for developing digital organizational resilience in government organizations"* (Fleron, et al. 2021). Moreover, for organizational resilience in general, they found that their study contributes a historical account of *"how large, federated organizations can grow resilience in the organizational network as a resilience ecosystem"* (p. 2408).

Denmark has also prioritized cyber defense in the military. On 28 January 2018, the Danish Government and a broad majority of the Danish Parliament agreed on a six-year Defence Agreement for the period 2018-2023. The new Defence Agreement has a particular focus on strengthening the following areas: 1) Denmark's contributing to NATOs collective deterrence and defence; 2) The

Armed Forces' ability and capacity to take part in international operations and stabilization efforts; 3) Contribution to national security, e.g., in the event of terror attacks in Denmark; 4) Protection of Denmark against cyber-attacks; 5) Improvement of the national emergency. The focus on cyber-attacks is of particular importance in light of the serious security and socioeconomic consequences from attacks faced by Denmark in cyberspace (Frederiksen, 2018).

The UK strategy for cyber resilience has been centered on four policy objectives: (1) ensuring the foundations are in place, so that organizations understand what 'good' looks like; (2) ensuring appropriate skills exist to implement this guidance; (3) creating better market incentives for investing in cyber risk management; and (4) improving accountability and responsibility across organizations (UK, 2020). The UK has used its global leadership role to support other countries building resilience in response to and recovery from major crises, such as COVID-19.

Recently, the UK has focused on boosting the resilience of its supply chain in light of the Solar Winds and Codecov attacks. The UK government has helped organizations improve their cyber risk management during the pandemic, including through £500,000 of funding to enable critical suppliers in healthcare to develop their preparedness and resilience. The UK through its National Centre on Cyber Security (NCCS) provides support to critical organizations in the UK, the wider public sector, industry, SMEs as well as the general public by providing effective incident response to minimize harm to the UK, help with recovery, and learn lessons for the future.

A survey of the threats from cyberspace by the Federal Office for Information Security (Bundesamt für Sicherheit in der Informationstechnik – BSI) reveals that in Germany alone, the overall economic losses caused by cybercrime have doubled to over EUR 100 billion in the last two years according to estimates provided by the digital association Bitkom (Gries, 2020). Cybercriminals have got their eye on the financial industry, and there are attacks on financial institutions almost on a daily basis. The German public perspective on the challenges, procedures, and instruments of cybersecurity follows three lines of development: First, the close link of cybersecurity with data protection and privacy issues; second, the distinct way of dealing with technical hazards by means of (regulatory and engineering) risk prevention mechanisms; and third, the debate on "digital sovereignty" that was triggered by the Snowden revelations. In light of growing political tensions between major powers such as the United States, Russia, and China, the German government, has called for collaboration with like-minded European and international organizations and sees the opportunity to take a leading role in reinvigorating an inclusive international effort to maintain peace and stability in cyberspace. Germany has in particular focused on cyber resilience within the banking industry. The regulatory changes suggested by EIOPA, the EBA and ESMA and the suggestion for a framework for cyber resilience testing are intended to contribute to the effective management of ICT risks as part of proper business organization, and therefore to an appropriate level of cyber resilience in regulated institutions (BaFin, 2021).

4.4. Global Internet Governance

Since the 1990s, various efforts have been made to construct an international regime for global Internet governance. Beginning with the formation of the Internet Corporation for Assigned Names and Numbers, efforts at regime construction were a main focus of the 2001–2005 UN World Summit on the Information Society (WSIS, 2005). However, little progress was made toward an international agreement. As the cyber resilience literature provides very little research on the role of governance in the development of cyber resiliency, this chapter introduces an important subject to the cyber taxonomy. Governance functions are a critical aspect of any cyber resilience system, including the requirement to designate resources to be secured; define organizational risk tolerance; set organizational priorities; and determine the security and resilience mechanisms to be employed within the methodology (NIST, 2018).

For example, the United States could not have anticipated, when the Internet was developed in the 1970s, the massive capacity for nation-states, governing bodies, non-state actors, local police, criminal actors, and private commerce connected to national security devices to conduct Internet surveillance. Nor could it have anticipated the resourcing required, or the potential for damage to national interests and national reputation created by massive exfiltration (Greiman, 2019).

Resilience requires more than just a risk management or tactical framework but must consider other elements of governance including resilience-related accountability, decision-making, environmental factors including cultural, political, and legal hazards, national goals, and change governance. The activities involved in governance are often confused with management activities. Governance is focused on providing oversight to the operational resilience management system, not performing, or managing process tasks to completion. For example, the process of overseeing the identification, definition, and inventorying of high-value assets is a governance task, while performing these tasks is part of operational resilience process management. Effective resilience process governance means that senior leadership (which typically includes boards of directors and higher-level managers) provides sponsorship and oversight to the process and provides direction and guidance on course correction when deemed necessary (Carnegie Mellon, 2016). This chapter identifies the forms of governance in cyberspace as it relates to maintaining resilient systems. In doing so, we determine commonalities and divergences between cyber structures and other enterprise-level governances. Then, we parse the relationships between these commonalities and divergences in order to examine resilience. If we understand governance as a separate concept from resilience, we have not only diluted the meaning of resilience, but we have also failed to recognize how governance drives resilience and ensures the sustainability of resilient systems in a networked world.

To fully understand the global impact of cyber resilience it is helpful to identify the various governance structures in the cyber realm but also develop a perspective on why governance matters in ensuring cyber resilience by tackling the following questions: What is the meaning of governance in the cyber literature? How are cyber governance and resilience connected at the national, transnational, and regional levels? Is governance generally recognized as a central component of national cyber security strategies? As shown in table 4.1, based on emerging concepts, principles and strategies for cyberspace, various models have developed for cyber governance promulgated by governments, the private sector, non-profits, academics, and inter-governmental organizations (Rustad, 2020; Maurer, 2020; NATO, 2017; NIST, 2018; OECD, 2019; European Commission, 2013; Solum, 2008; WSIS, 2005).

Table 4.1: *Cyber governance and resilience frameworks*

Cyber Governance	Characteristics	Selected Resilience Initiatives and Frameworks
Self- Governance	Decentralized, Deregulated, Uncensored, Voluntary, Bottom-Up, Laws, Norms, Architecture, Market Forces	The ability of a whole architecture to provide functional capabilities necessary for mission success despite environmental adversity or hostile action. Japan respects self-governance capabilities that the Internet has nurtured and regards every stakeholder's self-reliant activity for the Internet management as the basic foundation of cyber governance (Japan, 2015).
Transnational	Treaties, norms, cooperative problem-solving arrangements, soft power, networks, interlocking governance systems, monitoring, sanctions, dispute resolution systems, mix of multistake-holderism, nationalism and regionalism	The EU has developed Measurement Frameworks and Metrics for Resilient Networks and Services: Challenges and Recommendations (ENISA 2011b). Ensuring cyber resilience in NATO's command, control and communications systems is a top priority of NATO. Allies are committed to enhancing information-sharing and mutual assistance in preventing, mitigating, and recovering from cyber-attacks. (NATO, 2020). The ITU Global Cybersecurity Agenda includes cyber resilience in smart sustainable cities and identifies a framework consisting of five strategic pillars relevant to resilience: legal, technical, organizational, capacity-building, and cooperation (ITU, 2015). The OECD has developed resilience strategies and approaches to contain systemic threats (OECD, 2019).

Cyber Governance	Characteristics	Selected Resilience Initiatives and Frameworks
Polycentrism	Multilateralism, Organic adaptability, Accountability, Mutual adjustment, Private sector collaboration, Overlapping jurisdiction	Polycentrism focuses on the development of public private partnerships and development of an eco-structure that encourages self-reliance, and concern about others. Polycentric or multilateral resilience frameworks have been developed by the following organizations: NIST Framework information sharing and best practices, Cybersecurity Tech Accord 2020 in Review (CTA, 2021); Internet Engineering Task Force (IETF); Internet Research Task Force (IRTF) and The Paris Call for Trust and Security in Cyberspace (Paris, 2018).
Nationalism	Geographically bounded, single government, state-centric laws and frameworks, state control, top-down decision making, historic, cultural, and linguistic cohesiveness	Nationalism is evident in the growing industry related frameworks for cyber resilience such as Saudi Arabia's National Information Security Integrated Strategy (NISS); CISA (2020) in the U.S.; Singapore's cyber resilient infrastructure and workforce initiatives (Singapore, 2020); Israel's National Cyber Directorate (Israel, 2020); Cyber Security Law (China, 2017); Cyber Resilience Policy (UK Cyber Security Strategy, 2020).
Regionalism	Geographic contiguity, democratic, distributive, co-regulation, shared values and cultures, interaction, common political institutions, military interaction, norms pertaining to conflict resolution	The global financial system's operational cyber resilience and collective defense against cyber-attacks (Maurer and Nelson, 2020); the European Union's TIBER-EU; European Commission (EC) Digital Operational Resilience Act (DORA) (EC, 2019); the eGovernment initiatives for the Economic and Social Commission for Western Asia (ESCWA); the Financial Stability Board of the Bank for International Settlements Guidance on Cyber Resilience (BIS, 2016); the Budapest Cyber-Crime Convention; the African Union Convention on Cyber Security.

4.4.1. Self-Governance

Self-governance, sometimes referred to as distributive governance exists in many forms on the Internet and has drawn its inspiration from the theory and practice of the open governance movement (Barlow, 1996; Verhulst et al., 2014). Networked and Distributive Governance is intended to be in alignment with biological governance systems that have proven to be highly resilient. Networked and distributive governance of an organization's risk creates freedom to confidently take risk in pursuit of the ends or values (Koening, 2015). Richard Stallman, began the free software movement in the 1970s with the establishment of MIT's Artificial Intelligence Lab. To Stallman this was a moral obligation of all developers (Tsai, 2008).

Japan has recognized the importance of self-governance or distributive governance in its national cyber security strategy by recognizing that *"[t]he Internet has made progress powered by the self-governance of various participating actors.*

Even if cyber threats become national challenges requiring the nation's all-out efforts, it is possible, and appropriate as well, for a government to take all charges for maintaining order in cyberspace" (Japan, 2015). *"Japan respects self-governance capabilities that the Internet has nurtured and regards every stakeholder's self-reliant activity for the Internet management as the basic foundation of cyber governance. Thus, promoting the development and operation of a self-governance mechanism for the fulfillment of the functions and missions of various social systems connected to cyberspace, and for the deterrence of malicious cyber activities"* (Japan, 2015).

The characteristics of cyberspace reduce some of the power differentials among actors, and thereby provide a good example of the diffusion of power that typifies global politics. The largest powers such as transnational organizations are unlikely to be able to dominate this domain as much as they have others like sea or air (Nye, 2010). Researchers have helped to clarify the mechanisms that shape cyber power and demonstrate how mobile technologies create pressures on state control, and how the state responds to such pressures (Goldsmith and Wu, 2006).

4.4.2. Transnationalism

In recent years, a growing body of transnational cyber governance is represented by the evolution of multistakeholderism. The concept of multistakeholderism and the flexible Internet governance vision it embraces has evolved from its original structure as nations have expressed concern over a U.S. Centric governance structure, resulting in a transition plan to privatize the coordination and management of the Domain Name Severs (DNS), as discussed in the 2016 Congressional Research Service's Report on the Domain Name System (Kruger, 2016).

The Council of Europe (CoE) in its Internet Governance Strategy is firmly committed to, multistakeholder governance with leading actors in the field of Internet governance, including relevant international organizations, the private sector, and civil society. The Council of Europe promotes the full inclusion of all stakeholders, in their respective roles, in Internet governance and aims to ensure that public policy is people-centered respecting the core values of democracy, human rights and the rule of law. Austria, through its National Cyber Security Strategy (NCSS) emphasizes a multi-stakeholder approach through its strategic goals which include partnership or cooperation with stakeholders, including international organizations, local and regional governance, and through partnerships and knowledge sharing with the private sector (Austria, 2013). NATO has also begun to take a leading role in cyber resilience. At the Brussels Summit in 2018, Allies agreed to set up a new Cyberspace Operations Centre as part of NATO's strengthened Command Structure. They also agreed that NATO can draw on national cyber capabilities for its missions and operations.

Global transnational governance has become critical to national security and has emerged in various forms. The significance of global transnational governance is evidenced through the enactment of multinational and regional agreements and treaties that can impact cyberspace in a profound way. For example, the role of NATO, as described by Alexander Klimburg in the National Cyber Security Framework Manual, is designed to be a political-military alliance, with its interests coalescing around counter-crime, intelligence and counterintelligence, critical infrastructure protection and national crisis management, and diplomacy and internet governance among its 29 member nations (Klimburg, 2012). NATO is increasingly portrayed as if it were simply the armed wing of the European Union, committed not only to the welfare of North Atlantic populations, but also to the populations of neighboring territories. This ignores the fact that NATO boldly uses force in the service of protecting the economic and national security of the Alliance (NATO CCD COE, 2.0, 2017).

4.4.3. Polycentrism

Scholars that have explored the evolution of best practices for developing international cybersecurity legal frameworks and governance structures have recommended an on-going process and a dynamic "bottom up" approach (Satola and Judy, 2011). Others have recommended a more polycentric regime that includes private sector engagement and multilateral collaboration (McGinnis, 2016; Shackelford, et al., 2016).

Polycentricity has been defined as (1) multiple centers of decision-making authority with overlapping jurisdictions, (2) which interact through a process of mutual adjustment during which they frequently establish new formal collaborations or informal commitments, and (3) their interactions generate a regularized pattern of overarching social order which captures efficiencies of scale at all levels of aggregation, including providing a secure foundation for democratic self-governance (McGinnis, 2016). Kikuchi and Okubo (2020) through their examination of the importance of resilience and polycentric governance for cyberspace, identified three factors of polycentric governance that are critical for building resilience of cyberspace: eco structure, collaboration, and accountabilities.

"Polycentric initiatives applied to the cyber world recognizes both the common but differentiated responsibilities of public and private sector stakeholders as well as the potential for best practices to be identified and spread organically" (Shackelford, et al., 2016). Thus, polycentric governance involves notions of mutual adjustment, and organic adaptability. For example, best practices could be shared through initiatives such as the NIST Framework or public private collaboration at the local, national, and regional levels. Multilateralism appears in more recent discussions of polycentric approaches to governance that focus on knowledge sharing and public private sector collaborations. Since polycentric governance is an evolving domain, ontological development will require analyzing the models of multilateralism versus the models of multistakeholderism more commonly used in the transnational domain.

4.4.4. Nationalism

National governments continue to focus on the development of risk strategies, policies, and standards to protect critical infrastructure. National and international cyber security strategies aim to foster better relationships between the public and private sector and among nation-states. Recently, there has been a focus on national cyber security law that provides for stricter government controls over 'critical information infrastructure.' For example, China's government has approved a broad cybersecurity law aimed at tightening and centralizing state control over information flows and technology equipment, raising concerns among foreign companies operating in the country (KPMG, 2017; Chin and Dou, 2016). Under China's Cyber Security Law, the Cyber Resilience standards consist of seven aspects, which are personal information protection, critical information infrastructure, network operators, security capability requirements for big data services, sensitive information protection, certification of security products and legal liabilities (KPMG, 2017). Russia has also passed a law, which increases government access to online content (Russia, 2016). The Yarovaya law, as it is known, has been condemned by opposition and human rights activists, and even Edward Snowden, the fugitive NSA contractor who was granted asylum in Russia. But the legislation requires Russian citizens to inform the government whenever they believe they have "reliable" information on a possible terror attack, uprisings, and a slew of other crimes (Russia, 2016). In terms of nation-state activity, some cyber scholars claim, *"if the US government does not find a way to deter Russia's use of electronic disruption in support of its political agenda, it is likely that the latter will see this as an effective and penalty-free technique to be repeated elsewhere in the world"* (Wickett, 2017, p. 34).

In accordance with the United Nations Charter Article 51, official doctrine reserves the right to respond to a cyberattack by any means that are felt to be necessary and proportional. In the United States, high level government officials with national security and law enforcement agencies have argued that expanded surveillance powers are needed, especially because of the threat of small, deadly terrorist plots that are hard to detect,

As an example, to assist in coordination of a complex interconnected intelligence infrastructure consisting of 17 agencies and organizations, the White House appointed the first federal Chief Information Security Officer to drive cybersecurity policy, planning, and implementation across the Government under the 2016 Cybersecurity National Action Plan (WH, 2016). In 2018, the Cybersecurity and Infrastructure Security Agency (CISA) was established to build the national capacity to defend against cyber-attacks and work with the federal government to provide cybersecurity tools, sharing of information between the pubic and the private sector, incident response services and assessment capabilities to safeguard the '.gov' networks that support the essential operations of partner departments and agencies (DHS, 2020; CISA, 2015).

4.4.5. Regionalism

Regionalism is also of great significance in the development of international strategies for cyber resilience to better protect the financial systems and health care systems which operate on a global scale. COVID 19 for example, has created a need for resilience in our cyber systems due to increased cyber-attacks during the pandemic threatening the pharmaceutical industry, hospitals, and professionals in the health care field, not to mention the disruption of life saving medical treatments. Various frameworks for cyber resilience have been advanced at the regional level. Some examples include the G7 CEG (Cyber Export Group) which has issued fundamental principles, analyzed systemic risks, and conducted simulations

(Cyber Export Group, 2019). Another example is the Bank for International Settlements (BIS) establishment of its Cyber Resilience Coordination Centre (CRCC) (FSB, 2020).

The UN Department of Economic and Social Affairs (UNDESA) (2020) in its eGovernment Survey highlights many of the regional collaborations in digitization and cyber resilience. Digital trade, the digital economy and open government data are areas of regional focus among the member countries of the Economic Commission for Africa (ECA), the members of the Economic and Social Commission for Western Asia (ESCWA) and the Economic Commission for Europe (ECE). The role of digital government in disaster risk reduction has special relevance among the countries in the Economic and Social Commission for Asia and the Pacific (ESCAP) region; and the large-scale digitalization of core public sector functions and the adoption of strategic (rather than incremental or silo-based) policies and implementation plans are assigned primary importance among the country members of ESCAP and the Economic Commission for Latin America and the Caribbean (ECLAC).

One of the most advanced areas in regionalization as it relates to cyber security is the enforcement of international criminal law. There is a wide range of cyber threats, including war, espionage, sabotage, and disruption, (Rid, 2013) and international law is ambiguous about their status as a crime, an act of war, or act of espionage. Presently, there are seven major agreements governing cybercrime representing every region of the world, with the largest regional group represented by the Convention on Cybercrime popularly known as the Budapest Convention. The Convention has served as an important governance tool on many levels including through its mandatory provisions on the enactment of legislation to combat cybercrime, extradition, mutual assistance, and law enforcement (Convention, 2001).

These regional agreements play a significant role in cyber resilience and offer a more holistic approach to improving cyber relations among nations. However, there are many that believe the Convention on Cybercrime is stalemated by opposition from countries that use cybercrime as a political tool and by new powers who object to signing a treaty that they did not negotiate (CSIS, 2017). Cyber resilience will be impacted by the lack of harmonization and coordination of the criminal laws between nations (CSIS, 2017).

4.5. Governance through Cyber Laws and Regulations

Since cyberlaw plays a critical role in the implementation of cyber resilience programs globally it is important to recognize that nation states are beginning to develop new laws and revise existing laws to make sure there is strategic alignment between the law and required technical compliance. The principles and over-arching structure of global cyber law is drawn from decades of law making through international organizations including the UN Charter and NATO's North Atlantic Treaty, court decisions, customary law, statutes, and regulations, and more recently risk strategies, policies, and standards. The development of cyber law as an international body of law is complex and raises challenges for cyber-related contract law, tort law governing property rights and personal injury, privacy law, the prosecution of cyber-crimes, law enforcement, civil procedure, and intellectual property protection. However, the challenge still exists in enforcement as well as jurisdictional issues. A few examples of governance through regulation are set forth in the following sections.

4.5.1. Privacy Rights

One of the most important areas of regulation impacting cyber resilience is protecting the rights of billions of users around the globe through the regulation of privacy. Privacy rights can vary widely around the world. For example, the European Union enacted a strict Directive, the General Data Protection Directive (GDPD) giving citizens' back control of their data (EU GDPR, 2016), while the United States has left much of Internet privacy protection to state control which can vary widely, with some states offering greater protection than others. At the federal level, the Federal Trade Commission Act under (15 U.S. Code sec. 41 et seq.) broadly empowers the FTC to bring enforcement actions to protect consumers against unfair and deceptive practices and to enforce federal privacy and data protection regulations. Specific privacy regulations can be found for the health care and financial industries. Recent focus in the EU has been on data protection by design as a legal obligation for data controllers and processors, making an explicit reference to data minimization and the possible use of pseudonymization, and introduces the obligation of data protection by default, going a step further into stipulating the protection of personal data as a default property of systems and services (ENISA, 2018). Privacy in the EU is discussed further in Chapter 5.

4.5.2. Standards for Cyber Resilience

In recent years, organizations are showing increasing interest in the introduction of internationally recognized standards for cyber resilience and security. In Europe, ENISA has been active in the field of standardization since its creation by cooperating with European and International Standards Organizations (ESOs and SDOs) in the area of NIS standardization. One of the first deliverables summarized and presented findings covering the importance of correctly defining resilience in the context of standardization, the identification and presentation of the major activities undertaken by Standards Developing Organizations (SDOs) in security, and identification of key areas where further work is necessary (ENISA, 2011b). The Regulation (EU) 2019/881 (Cybersecurity Act), establishes a European cybersecurity certification framework for ICT products, services, and processes. ENISA participates in this new framework, by preparing candidate certification schemes on the request of the European Commission or the European Cybersecurity Coordination Group (representation of Member States). Standardization is playing an important role in the framework, as the Act states the following:

There is a need for closer international cooperation to improve cybersecurity standards, including the need for definitions of common norms of behavior, the adoption of codes of conduct, the use of international standards, and information sharing, promoting swifter international collaboration in response to network and information security issues and promoting a common global approach to such issues.

The European Commission in December 2020 issued a new standard setting law-the Digital Services Act (DSA) for comment (EC, 2020b). This Act builds on the rules of the E-Commerce Directive, and addresses the issues emerging around online intermediaries. Member States have regulated these services differently, creating barriers for smaller companies looking to expand and scale up across the EU and resulting in different levels of protection for European citizens (ECDSA, 2020). Whereas the GDPR harmonized and raised data protection standards, the DSA aims to establish a comprehensive framework for how digital services operate in Europe to address among other factors illegal content and societal harm (Blankertz and Jaurscho, 2020).

The move toward bottom-up regulatory frameworks is best evidenced by the 2018 National Institute for Standards and Technology (NIST) Cybersecurity Framework, which aims to improve private sector cybersecurity through voluntary standards. The Framework integrates industry standards and best practices to help organizations manage their cybersecurity risks. It provides a common language that allows staff at all levels within an organization—and at all points in a supply chain—to develop a shared understanding of their cybersecurity risks. NIST worked with private-sector and government experts to create the Framework, which was first released in early 2014 and updated in 2018 (NIST, 2018). The effort went so well that Congress ratified it as a NIST responsibility in the Cybersecurity Enhancement Act of 2014. The Framework helps companies respond to and recover from cybersecurity incidents, prompting them to analyze root causes and consider how they can make improvements. Companies from around the world have embraced the use of the Framework, including JP Morgan Chase, Microsoft, Boeing, Intel, Bank of England, Nippon Telegraph and Telephone Corporation, and the Ontario Energy Board. Similarly, the Federal Financial Institutions Examination Council (FFIEC) provides a *"repeatable and measurable process for financial institutions to measure their cybersecurity preparedness over time."* Like the NIST RMF, the FFIEC CAT offers core principles and goals but relies on the company's own risk-management assessment and strategies. (FFIEC, 2017).

4.5.3. Reasonable Cyber Security Standards

Legislatures have struggled with the idea of whether to create a duty of reasonable security as the wrongful use of the Internet expands. Many regulators expect regulated companies to have implemented "reasonable" security measures, taking into account factors such as the sensitivity of the data protected. In the United States, in the absence of a federal law, the question of whether a company or organization has exercised "reasonable" cyber security practices has been the purview of the Federal Trade Commission. As an example, in August 2013, the U.S. Federal Trade Commission brought an administrative action against LabMD, Inc., a small, little-known medical testing company in Atlanta, Georgia, alleging violations of the Act in connection with alleged security breaches in 2008 and 2012.

The Commission's legal argument against Lab MD was their failure to employ *"reasonable and appropriate measures"* to protect consumers' information constituted an "unfair" act or practice under Section 5 of the FTC Act (Lab MD, 2013). On appeal to the 11th Circuit, the Court held that the cease-and-desist order contains no prohibitions. It does not instruct LabMD to stop committing a specific act or practice. Rather, it commands LabMD to overhaul and replace its data security program to meet an indeterminable standard of reasonableness. This command is unenforceable and lacks a penalty clause if they fail to act. The Eleventh Circuit acknowledged that due to limitations on legislating *"an extensive list of unfair acts or practices,"* Congress authorized the FTC *"to establish unfair acts or practices through case-by-case litigation."* Notably, the court did not squarely address the issue of whether the FTC has data security enforcement authority under section 5(a) (Lab MD, 2018). The court instead found that *"the [FTC's] complaint alleges no specific unfair acts or practices"* by LabMD other than the installation of P2P software on a single LabMD computer.

4.5.4.   *A Global Standard for Cyber Resilience Governance*

The major information cyber-attacks in recent years demonstrate that companies worldwide including those in the cyber security business are not prepared to manage the security of the Cloud even when compliance controls exist, and vendor support is in place. This was magnified in the recent Solar Winds case in the United States where the country's largest multinationals and the U.S. government were caught off guard by an attack on their cyber security vendor (Constantin, 2020). Many cyber incidents show that companies worldwide are not properly adapted to use and to manage the security of new cloud computing environments, even when compliance controls do exist, and vendor guidance is in place to provide support to companies and secure their environments.

From a global perspective, regulatory agencies must ensure that proper compliance frameworks and regulations are established to support local companies. For example, in many of the lesser developed countries in Africa and Latin America the absence of legislation enforcing the use of well-stablished standards such as the NIST or ISO frameworks means that companies based in these regions are not required to implement such controls that would prevent further incidents - except when the organization itself takes the initiative to apply such frameworks on their own. Cyber security requirements vary widely from on country to another creating a snowball effect when a business in one country with weak or no regulation is hit with a major cyber-attack that rapidly spreads to other businesses through the interconnectedness of their wider systems. However, these standards lack controls as complete and comprehensive as NIST.

The reality that many companies operate globally with customers and supply chains potentially anywhere in the world, it is critical that companies adopt global governance frameworks that feature cyber security controls capable of addressing the ever-changing technology. A global standard for cyber security governance is becoming an urgent matter that requires the attention and focus of every national government. The call for a bilateral or multilateral agreement is becoming closer to reality as we continue to witness the emerging global cyber crisis.

4.5.5.   *Bilateral and Multilateral Treaties*

Both China and the United States advocate for cyber governance rules domestically and internationally, but their contrasting approaches to these governance issues always breed misunderstandings and arouse suspicions on the other side (Levite and Jinghua, 2019). For example, cyber sovereignty as put forward by China does not mechanically apply the traditional concept to cyberspace. Instead, it views sovereignty as the respect for the right of each government to choose its own path for cyber development and internet policy. Its conception of cyber sovereignty does, in fact, go much further to assert the right of all nations to equally participate in cyber governance, to oppose cyber hegemony, and reject any interference through the internet in the internal affairs of other countries (Yeli, 2017). It disapproves conducting, indulging, and supporting any actions that may endanger other countries' cybersecurity (Second World Internet Conference, 2015). International treaties in the cyber realm have been discussed for decades among scholars, national governments, and private industry and though progress has been made (Goldsmith, 2011), to date other than the regional cyber-crime conventions a treaty governing cyber security and cyber resilience is still an aspiration. The major hurdles to a cybersecurity treaty appear to be (1) the lack of mutual interest; the problems the United States has in making concessions adequate to gain reciprocal benefits; and (3) the problem of verification (Goldsmith, 2011). Investment in research, education, technology, and identification of best practices are essential to reaching the long-term goal of cyber peace among nations supported by a global cyber treaty.

4.6. Summary

This chapter highlighted the need for better cyber governance at the local, national, transnational, and regional levels. Though progress has been made the number and the breadth of cyber-attacks remains alarming. The investigation of cyber-attacks shows that the world still needs better harmonization of the laws and common standards so that an incident in one country that has a less resilient governance system cannot impact countries where cyber resilience is a high priority. This requires laws, capacity, and infrastructure across the globe. The chapters that follow set forth model frameworks for building cyber resilient systems across industries and countries and provide insights into some of the more viable strategic, operational, and tactical methodologies for managing the dangers lurking in cyberspace.

Chapter 5

The United States and European Frameworks for Resilience

Threat is a mirror of security gaps. Cyber-threat is mainly a reflection of our weaknesses. An accurate vision of digital and behavioral gaps is crucial for a consistent cyber-resilience.

Stéphane Nappo - Global Head Information Security Société Générale

The goal of this chapter is to examine the resilience frameworks presently existing in the European Union and the United States, considered to be the most advanced in implementing cyber frameworks for resilience and security. The following are key questions that are raised in this research:

- To what extent have the United States and the European Union established a comprehensive framework for resilience at the local, national, and international level?
- What form does the framework take and how is it shaped?
- How does the framework adapt to the changing environment of cyberspace?
- How do they measure and evaluate the framework to determine if it is accomplishing its intended goals?

5.1. The United States

5.1.1. The United States Government Resilience Strategy and Framework

Despite the national and international importance, resilience metrics to inform management decisions are still in the early stages. Though much of the U.S. government, with the exception of the Military Branch, views resilience as a more tactical operation, by advancing strategies through tactical planning (U.S., HHS, 2017), the research in this book reflects a much broader meaning of resilience that emanates from long term strategic planning that is sensitive to the various ways our systems can be attacked and is responsive to emerging disruptive technologies that will be incorporated into our future modes of communication.

Most definitions of resilience do not incorporate the expansion of recent technologies including robotics, artificial intelligence, control systems, the Internet of things (IoT), crypt analysis or universal quantum computing. Nor does an understanding of resilience incorporate the human factors such as economic behavior, decision making, empowerment, capability, conflict resolution, incentives, integrity, orientation, perception, assumptions, critical thinking, systems thinking, among many other attributes that contribute to resilience. Remarkably, the Department of Defense Science Board uses the term cyber resilience or resilience 44 times in its Task Force Report on Cyber Deterrence without defining the meaning of "cyber resilience" indicating there is no standard taxonomic understanding of resilience across the Department of Defense (Defense Science Board, 2017). Further elaboration of the views of the Department of Defense on cyber resilience is discussed in chapter 6.

To improve cyber resilience and the security of infrastructure to a wide range of threats, the White House issued an Executive Order in 2021 on improving the Nation's Cyber Security. The important provisions include (1) removing barriers to sharing threat information; (2) enhanced software supply chain security; (3) strict cyber incident reporting; and (4) partnering with the private sector (WH, 2021).

To focus on antiquated systems in an organized way, on May 11, 2017, Presidential Executive Order 13800 on Strengthening the Cybersecurity of Federal Networks and Critical Infrastructure was issued by President Trump (WH, 2017). Accountability of government agency heads was an important theme of the Order, and the Framework for Improving Critical Infrastructure Cybersecurity (the Framework) developed by the National Institute of Standards and Technology (NIST), is the benchmark for measuring cyber resilience in the federal government (NIST, 2018). The Secretary of Homeland Security and the Director of the White House Office of Management and Budget (OMB), consistent with chapter 35, subchapter II of title 44, United States Code, oversees compliance and enforcement of these standards making it the policy of the executive branch to build and maintain a modern, secure, and more resilient executive branch IT architecture (WH, 2017). Presidential Policy Directive (PPD-41) (WH, 2016a) sets forth principles and processes to guide the government's response to information security incidents in both the public and private sectors. PPD-41 clearly articulates incident response processes and outlines the responsibilities of key agencies and entities across the government, including OMB, DHS, NSC, FBI, and the Intelligence Community. PPD-41 also promotes a well-coordinated response that brings to bear the capabilities of the federal government to mitigate the damage of cybersecurity incidents and enable the restoration and recovery of affected systems.

In 2018 a new National Cyber Strategy was implemented by the Executive Office of the White House to increase the security and resilience of the Nation's information and information systems. This strategy has the following key priorities: (1) Secure Federal networks and information. (2) Secure critical infrastructure. (3) Combat cybercrime and improve incident reporting (WH, 2018).

5.1.2. Cyberspace Solarium Commission

Two years after the implementation of the new cyber strategy, a congressionally mandated report was released in March of 2020 which described a new strategy to reduce the likelihood and impact of significant cyberattacks on the United States. The report was conducted by the Cyberspace Solarium Commission, a bipartisan organization created in the 2019 defense policy bill to develop a multipronged U.S. cyber strategy (Cyberspace (CSC) Report, 2020). The approach, dubbed "layered cyber deterrence" calls for stronger public-private collaboration, reducing vulnerabilities and broader adoption of a Department of Defense concept of working in foreign networks to confront cyber threats as far away from American infrastructure as possible. Specifically, the strategy relies on three efforts: (1) Shaping behavior: America should work with other nations to promote responsible behavior in cyberspace; (2) Denying benefits: The strategy requires the U.S. to deny benefits to adversaries who have long exploited cyberspace to America's disadvantage at little cost to themselves. This requires securing critical networks in collaboration with the private sector to promote national resilience and increase the security of the cyber ecosystem; and (3) Imposing costs: The United States must be able to retaliate against those that target the nation in cyberspace. The Commission Report has six pillars which include (1) reform the U.S. government structure and organization for cyberspace; (2) strengthen norms and non-military tools; (3) promote national resilience; (4) reshape the cyber eco system toward greater security; (5) operationalize cyber security collaboration with the private sector; and (6) preserve and employ the military instrument of power (U.S. CSC Report, 2020). With the passage of the FY2021 National Defense Authorization Act, 25 of the Commission's 80 recommendations have been codified into law (HR, 2021). A key provision of the Bill is the reestablishment of cybersecurity leadership in the White House by creating a national cyber director position.

5.1.3.   Homeland Security

The Blueprint for a Secure Cyber Future builds on the Department of Homeland Security Quadrennial Review Report's strategic framework by providing a clear path to create a safe, secure, and resilient cyber environment for the homeland security enterprise (DHS, 2014). With this guide, stakeholders at all levels of government, the private sector, and international partners can work together to develop the cybersecurity capabilities that are key to our economy, national security, and public health and safety. The Blueprint describes two areas of action: (1) Protecting our critical information infrastructure today; and (2) building a stronger cyber ecosystem for tomorrow. The Blueprint is designed to protect the United States 'most vital systems and assets and, over time, drive fundamental change in the way people and devices work together to secure cyberspace. The Blueprint lists four goals for protecting critical information infrastructure: (1) Reduce Exposure to Cyber Risk; (2) Ensure Priority Response and Recovery; (3) Maintain Shared Situational Awareness; and (4) Increase Resilience. Achieving a safe, secure, and resilient cyber environment includes measuring progress in building capabilities and determining whether they are effective in an evolving threat environment. Accordingly, each year's performance is compared with that of the previous year. In addition, the National Cybersecurity and Communications Integration Center (NCCIC) serves as a 24/7 cyber monitoring, incident response, and management center and as a national point of cyber and communications incident integration.

The Stakeholder Engagement and Cyber Infrastructure Resilience (SECIR) division is the Department of Homeland Security's (DHS) primary point of engagement and coordination for national security/emergency preparedness (NS/EP) communications and cybersecurity initiatives for both government and industry partners. The Federal Network Resilience (FNR) Division of Homeland Security is responsible for developing innovative approaches to drive change in cybersecurity risk management by focusing on establishing metrics that have measurable impact on improving cybersecurity for federal civilian executive branch departments and agencies; gathering cybersecurity requirements and developing operational policies for the federal government; collaborating with, and providing outreach to, the Office of Management and Budget (OMB), the Federal Chief Information Officer (CIO) Council, and individual agency Chief Information (CIOs) and Chief Information Security Officers (CISOs); and leveraging best practices across CS&C and lessons learned in support of federal civilian executive branch departments' and agencies' cyber hygiene.

5.1.4. National Institute of Standards and Technology

The NIST Standards for resilience are widely recognized and adopted around the globe. Somewhat uniquely among the frameworks researched, protecting civil liberties is a stated goal for this framework. In the United States, the Department of Commerce's National Institute of Standards and Technology (NIST) has issued regulations that include the government's risk-based approach to cybersecurity. However, while a national mandate exists, individual federal agencies vary widely in implementation strategies, methodologies, and maturity. The standards set forth the policy on critical infrastructure. To better address these risks, the President issued Executive Order 13636, "Improving Critical Infrastructure Cybersecurity," on February 12, 2013, which established that *"[i]t is the Policy of the United States to enhance the security and resilience of the Nation's critical infrastructure and to maintain a cyber environment that encourages efficiency, innovation, and economic prosperity while promoting safety, security, business confidentiality, privacy, and civil liberties."* In enacting this policy, the Executive Order calls for the development of a voluntary risk-based Cybersecurity Framework – a set of industry standards and best practices to help organizations manage cybersecurity risks. The term resilience is used 7 times in the Framework but is never formally defined within the document or in the glossary attached to the document. The Framework enables organizations – regardless of size, degree of cybersecurity risk, or cybersecurity sophistication – to apply the principles and best practices of risk management to improving the security and resilience of critical infrastructure.

5.1.5. Nation-States

Nation-states can be strengthened through regionalism and globalization, however, the concern for national security can lead to the decline of globalization as evidenced by increasing national focus on safeguarding the nation, the building of public private partnerships, and increased protectionism in national cyber security strategies and legal frameworks. For example, the United States has passed several laws to enhance national security including appointing the first federal Chief Information Security Office to drive cybersecurity policy, planning, and implementation across the Government under the White House Cybersecurity National Action Plan (WH, 2016). The U.S. National Cybersecurity Information Sharing Act (CISA) also provides important tools necessary to strengthen the Nation's cybersecurity through public private collaboration, particularly by making it easier for private companies to share cyber threat information with each other and the Government (CISA, 2015), and the first Report on Securing and Growing the Digital Economy was released by the Commission on Enhancing National Cybersecurity recommending six imperatives to advance cyber security and safeguard the nation (WH, 2016b). Information-sharing among private and public stakeholders is a powerful mechanism to better understand a constantly changing environment. Information-sharing is a form of strategic partnership among key public and private stakeholders and also an important source for maintaining cyber resilience.

5.2. The European Union

5.2.1. The European Resilience Framework

According to the European Economic and Social Committee, cybercrime continues to grow as society becomes increasingly digitized. The EU is a highly attractive target for cybercrime in all its forms, because of its high level of internet penetration (73%) and advanced internet mediated services. (Socta, 2017). Moreover, in such an interconnected world, an attack on one business can harm many others.

To prevent this, the European Commission has been working on a cyber resilience framework and released its global strategy for the EU's Foreign and Security Policy in June 2016 (EU Global Strategy, 2016). An important component of the Strategy was its increased focus on cyber security by "*equipping the EU and assisting Member States in protecting themselves against cyber threats while maintaining an open, free and safe cyberspace*" (pp. 21-22). As stated in the Strategy this entails "*strengthening the technological capabilities aimed at mitigating threats and the resilience of critical infrastructure, networks, and services, and reducing cybercrime*" (pp. 21-22). Further, The EU will support political, operational, and technical cyber cooperation between Member States, and will enhance its cyber security cooperation with core partners such as the US and NATO, develop strong public-private partnerships, foster a common cyber security culture, and raise preparedness for possible cyber disruptions and attacks. In the implementation of the EU Global Strategy, "*[t]he European Union adopts a transformational approach to resilience, aimed at protecting rights, building political participation, fostering sustainable development and security. The goal is to do so in a manner that enables states and societies to withstand, adapt, recover and respond to shocks and crises if and when they arise*" (EC, 2017c).

As a key component of its *Shaping Europe's Digital Future*, the Recovery Plan for Europe, and the EU Security Union Strategy, the 2020 European Cyber Strategy will bolster Europe's collective resilience against cyber threats and help to ensure that all citizens and businesses can fully benefit from trustworthy and reliable services and digital tools. Whether it is the connected devices, the electricity grid, or the banks, planes, public administrations, and hospitals Europeans deserve to do so with the assurance that they will be shielded from cyber threats. Furthermore, the Commission is making proposals to address both cyber and physical resilience of critical entities and networks (EC, 2020a). George Christou in his systematic study on cyber security from the perspective of the EU analyzed the kind of resilience model the EU should develop. He underlines that this is a complex and multilayered issue, necessitating an interdisciplinary approach (Christou, 2016, p. 7).

However, many cybersecurity strategies within and beyond Europe refer to developing effective cyber resilience, but without adequately defining and deconstructing what resilience is, what it looks like at different stages, and the preconditions and governance forms required to achieve it. Approaches to cybersecurity thus far have been theoretically and conceptually eclectic but remain the basis for developing a strong cyber resilience.

5.2.2. *Cyber Security as Resilience: Cyber Security Policy*

In the EU, cybersecurity policy is a 'shared area of competence' between Member States and the EU, which implies that when the EU decides to regulate, EU law takes primacy over any adopted national law. To improve the operational and tactical levels of cybersecurity, the 2016 European Commission Communication *"Strengthening Europe's Cyber Resilience System and Fostering a Competitive and Innovative Cybersecurity Industry"* required Member States to transpose the Directive on Security of Network and Information Systems (NIS, Directive 3) cooperation mechanisms and to enhance cross-border cooperation related to preparedness for a large-scale cyber incident (EC, 2021a).

The NIS Directive is the first piece of EU-wide legislation on cybersecurity which provides legal measures to boost the overall level of cybersecurity in the EU. The Directive provides for a coordinated approach to crisis cooperation across the various elements of the cyber ecosystem that would increase preparedness and also ensure synergies and coherence with existing crisis management mechanisms (EC, 2021a). Among its important provisions is the establishment of an EU Cybersecurity Crisis Response Framework that requires the testing of procedures within the Framework and that *"Member States and the EU Institutions should regularly practice at the national and European level, including their political response, where necessary and with the involvement of private sector entities as appropriate"* (EC, 2017c). Moreover, the Directive provides that Member States, with the assistance of ENISA should cooperate in developing and adopting a common taxonomy and template for situational reports to describe the technical causes and impacts of cybersecurity incidents to further enhance their technical and operational cooperation during crises.

Throughout the EU, information sharing has been recognized strongly and encouraged between countries. As recognized by European network for Information Security Agency (ENISA), *"owners of critical infrastructures could potentially share with public authorities their input on mitigating emerging risks, threats, and vulnerabilities while public stakeholders could provide on a 'need to know basis' information on aspects related to the status of national security, including findings based on information collected by intelligence and cyber-crime units. Combining both views gives a very powerful insight on how the threat landscape evolves"* (ENISA, 2016b).

However, a study conducted in 2015 (Galexia, 2015) on EU cybersecurity maturity level showed a discrepancy between European countries at different levels. For instance, if most of them have a national cybersecurity strategy in place, only a few have a policy that requires (at least) an annual cybersecurity audit. Although it is possible to point to general trends and patterns of resilience in these cyber strategies, it is difficult to measure and assess conditions for resilience directly or indeed accurately – in particular in terms of cultural transformation in practice.

5.3. Security as Resilience Logic

Such general problems with measuring resilience in security contexts are compounded even further in the field of cybersecurity given the multitude of layers, levels, spaces, and dimensions that need to be measured.

The EU approach thus far, as defined in its cybersecurity strategy and in its practice, is underpinned predominantly by security as resilience logic; that of self-protection through development and projection of soft power (protective defence) and not hard power (offence). However, despite the EU's general orientation, the management of risks related to information and data assurance processes is also visible in its policies and platforms, and that of its member states. Traditional risk methodologies, despite their widespread use in cybersecurity, are incompatible with a security as resilience approach (socio-ecological). Such methodologies fit with the engineering definition of resilience that assume linearity and predictability but are fundamentally flawed in the context of complex networks and risks where uncertainty mitigates any accurate prediction of events (Dunn Cavelty and Prior, 2013). This said, the EU through initiatives such as the NISP, and its attempts to incentivize and create sustainable partnerships and working systems for information sharing and reporting, as well as operational aspects of cybercrime, have demonstrated that the EU is framing and constructing its actions within a security as resilience logic.

The Joint Communication on Cyber Resilience, Deterrence and Defence to the European Parliament and the Council on September 13, 2017, recognized cybersecurity as a common societal challenge, requiring multiple layers of government, economy and societal involvement. To address these concerns, the Cybersecurity Act (Regulation (EU) 2019/881), establishes a European cybersecurity certification framework for ICT products, services, and processes (EC, 2017a).

The EU's vision is that as the number of cyber-attacks increases and the issue becomes critical, considering the increasing digitalization of exchanges and the Internet of Things, a strong cyber resilience can only be built collectively on the basis of common policies using common frameworks and tools. Beyond nations and public institutions, these tools should be able to help companies build their cyber resilience, which will also protect citizens, who are also consumers.

5.3.1. Privacy Rights and Resilience

Indeed, a particularity of the EU's emerging ecosystem for cybersecurity is that it is centered on a specific type or notion of security as resilience, underpinned by concern not for national security of the state but security of the individual in cyberspace. Christou argues that thus far, the EU's cyber-security strategy aims much more at self-protection and promoting freedom of expression and human rights than at cyber hard power, in contrast to the United States (p. 1009). It can be explained by the fact that France and then Europe have always been sensitive to the protection of personal data. It is the primary mission of the Commission on Information Technology and Liberties (Commission Nationale de l'Informatique et des Libertés-CNIL) which is the regulator of personal data. Created in 1978, it assists professionals in their compliance and helps individuals to control their personal data and exercise their rights.

In 1995, the European Union adopted a directive (updated in 2012) designed to harmonize within the 28 Member States the protection afforded to all persons wherever in Europe their personal data are processed. Personal data protection is therefore at the heart of any reflection on cyber security in Europe, reinforced more recently with the GDPR, effective May 25, 2018, across the European Union. The GDPR affects all businesses that operate within the EU, regardless of where they are based. This new European regulation is in line with the French Data Protection Act of 1978 and strengthens citizens' control over the use that can be made of their data. The GDPR applies to any organization, public or private, that processes personal data on its own behalf or not, as long as it is established on the territory of the European Union, or has an activity directly targeting European residents.

Privacy is an essential element for resilience under the law. It requires that individuals must give their consent for organizations to process their personal data. They also have the right to opt out of activity from online companies, to refuse any sort of profiling and to file a complaint if the data subject considers that the processing of personal data relating to him or her infringes this Regulation (Art. 77). Companies have thus to show their customers that their data is collected for specified, explicit and legitimate purposes and not further processed in a manner that is incompatible with those purposes (ART 5-b). This point is particularly important as it forces companies to be more transparent about data treatment by third parties. In addition, the Right to be Forgotten, has effectively been implemented in the EU. This means users have the right to request to have data erased, prevent its processing, or to have it removed if it is no longer necessary for its original sourcing purpose. This regulation answers growing concerns from European citizens. In France, the CNIL received 14,137 complaints in 2020 alone, a good part of them being complaints concerning the dissemination of personal data on the Internet. A major question for resilience will be a determination where the data is stored, and the operational requirements. Compliance obligations are states responsibility as they "*shall provide for one or more independent public authorities to be responsible for monitoring the application of this Regulation*" (Art 51.1). This applies across industries including technology, financial services, for which a specific framework is being tested in Europe, health care, energy, and education.

Europe takes privacy rights very seriously and want companies to be held accountable. Companies are responsible for the data they store and use and must ensure their safety. Moreover, the European Union cybersecurity legislation makes it mandatory for any company to notify the supervisory authority no later than 72 hours after having become aware of a data breach. If a company has its data hacked, it must declare it, and will receive a penalty. According to the regulation, "*the amount of the fines will vary depending on the nature, severity and duration of the breach and taking into account the scope or purpose of the processing involved, as well as the number of individuals affected and the level of harm they have suffered*". Whenever a breach takes place in the context of cross-border processing and notification is required, the controller will need to notify the lead supervisory authority.

5.4. Summary

This chapter presented resilience frameworks presently existing in the European Union and the United States. The evolution of the frameworks was shown in response to the changing environment of cyber space and its reaction to internal and external events. The recently proposed new strategy in the U.S. will focus on changing behaviors, imposing costs on wrongful behavior, and focusing on national resilience. Similar to the U.S. the European Union's new strategy is also focused on national resilience as well as their long-standing commitment to the protection of privacy and human rights in cyberspace.

Chapter 6

Resilience on the Battlefield: Cyber-attack as an Act of War

Know the Enemy, Know Yourself, Know the Battlefield

Sun Tsu, The Art of War

In this chapter, the cyber defense strategies of various military organizations are analyzed, including the U.S. Department of Defense's limited but specific role to withstand a potential attack if it penetrates the United States' defenses (DoD, 2016). We also review the recent changes in cyber defense in the European Union. Cyber defense as an act of war is discussed not only in terms of the United States' role in defending the nation, but also in relationship to the role of NATO in establishing resilience as a core element of collective defense (Shea, 2017) as well as the role of cyber defense in the EU.

6.1. Cyber Defense in Europe

If the United States is capable of centralizing responses to cyber-attacks, it is different for the European Union. The EU comprises twenty-seven Member States of different sizes and with different modes of institutional organization. Each of these states is a sovereign state and coordinating the response to cyber threats is all the more complicated, but necessary, as the interdependence of European states at the economic, political, social, and military levels is obvious. The EU does not have its own army, and any intervention at the European level requires a strong coordination of its member states. It is the same for cyber defense, and offensive cyber capabilities have not been developed, or deployed, under the EU banner (Röhrig, 2015). It is therefore crucial to know what each Member State can deploy in terms of prevention and joint response. According to the European Parliament, almost all Member States have adopted a national cyber security strategy, and around 15 member states have included a military perspective of cyber defence in their national approaches, but only "*a few admit to investing in cyber weapons or define cyberspace as a potential warfare domain*" (Latici 2020).

The EU cyber response capabilities are therefore not led by the military. The EU has adopted a common civilian and military approach to self-protection in cyber space (Röhrig, 2015), considering the fact that military operations heavily rely on civilian actors, they could be impacted the same way and thus must work on the same cyber protection policy. As the synergies are obvious, working together will ensure that EU has the latest technology to face cyber-attacks.

6.1.1. EU Cyber Defense

Most types of cyber-attacks cannot be stopped or undone. Based on this fact, the EU strategy has been to adopt a preventative approach, rather than a reactive one. The majority of the actions implemented therefore seek to maximize security and minimize risk. The resources will therefore be developed in this direction and will focus on two aspects: 1) strengthening the security of the information systems and networks of all EU institutions, and 2) improving the cybersecurity of the entire Union, focusing on the networks and systems of its Member States.

EU member states agreed on the EU Concept for Cyber Defense in EU-led operations in 2012 allowing operational commanders to create and maintain situational cyber awareness. To support this concept on 18 November 2014 the EU Cyber Defence Policy Framework (CDPF) was adopted by the European Council and since then, through its implementation, concrete outputs have contributed to significantly enhance Member States' cyber defence capabilities. The Framework was updated in 2018. Six priority areas have been identified in the updated CDPF. A primary focus of this policy framework is the development of cyber defence capabilities, as well as the protection of the EU CDPF communication and information networks. Other priority areas include training and exercises, research and technology, civil-military cooperation, and international cooperation. It is also important that the cyber dimension is adequately addressed in exercises in order to improve the EU's ability to react to cyber and hybrid crises by improving decision-making procedures and availability of information (CDPF, 2018).

The EU Cybersecurity Strategy insists on the importance of cooperation between member States as its objective is to strengthen Europe's resilience against cyber threats and to ensure that all citizens and businesses can fully benefit from reliable and trustworthy digital services and tools.

To do so, the EU is working on a number of fronts to strengthen cyber resilience, fight cybercrime, boost cyber diplomacy, strengthen cyber defense, stimulate research and innovation and protecting critical infrastructure. As most of these actions show, the main objective is prevention and coordination.

6.1.2. Prevention and Coordination Agencies

To facilitate the development of a common cybersecurity policy, the EU has created in 2004 the European Union Agency for Cybersecurity (Regulation (EC) No 460/2004), that aims to develop throughout Europe the culture of security of information systems. The ENISA acts in support of public policy development, facilitating collaboration between member states and beyond, and actively contributing to the collection of intelligence to prepare for attacks. It assists the Commission and the Member States in achieving the level of information systems security required by the adopted directives. For example, ENISA encouraged and advised governments to set up CERTs (*Computer Emergency Response Team*), and then introduced Pan-European Cybersecurity Exercises to assess the level of collaboration and coordination of cybersecurity capabilities at the European level (Joubert & Samaan, 2014). By spreading a culture of cybersecurity, and by informing states, companies and individuals of the risks involved, ENISA is a major player in Europe for cyber resilience.

To go further in its ability to prevent and manage crises, the Commission has been working on a new Joint Cyber Unit, "*to strengthen cooperation between EU bodies and Member, State authorities responsible for preventing, deterring and responding to cyber-attacks, including civilian, law enforcement, diplomatic and cyber defense communities*" (EC, 2020). In April 2021, the Council agreed to the establishment of a Cybersecurity Competence Centre to pool investment in cybersecurity research, technology, and industrial development. The new organization, *the European Cybersecurity Industrial, Technology and Research Competence Centre*, will work in cooperation with a network of national coordination centers designated by the Member States and will allocate cybersecurity-related funding from the Horizon Europe program and the Digital Europe program. The ENISA will from now on focus on standards, and the European Council says the European Cyber Security Centre will be "*the EU's main instrument for pooling investment in cyber security research, technology and industrial development.*" Although not a formal EU agency, the European Cybersecurity Centre will be responsible for funding new cybersecurity research, providing financial support and technical assistance to cybersecurity start-ups and SMEs, and promoting its standards.

6.1.3. Response to Cyber Threats

In order to prepare and respond to cyber threats, the EU relies on two main structures, the European Defense Agency (EDA) and Europol. Created in July 2004, the European Defense Agency is an agency of the European External Action Service responsible for implementing European defense policy in terms of developing operational capabilities, its industrial and technological base, R&D programs, and cooperation in the field of armaments. It helps its 26 member States (all EU countries except Denmark) to develop their military resources and ensure the availability of proactive and reactive cyber defense technology. The Agency is active in the fields of cyber defense capability development and in Research & Technology (EDA, 2021). The purpose is to foster collaboration between the member States, providing virtual cyber defense training and exercise ranges for national cyber defense specialists training.

The EU's focus on cybersecurity is consistent with its model, which gives greater importance to police cooperation than to defense cooperation. Nevertheless, cyber defense is increasingly being discussed within the European Union, even though it faces several difficulties. Beyond the technical difficulty of tracing and attributing the source of the attack, there is the legal challenge. Legislation in the cyber domain is still too new for most states. This not only means that legislation differs from country to country, but also that the level of maturity in this aspect differs greatly from one country to another. Moreover, governance will vary from country to country. For example, coordination of the cyber security policy in the Netherlands is provided by the Ministry of Security and Justice, by the Ministry of Defense in Denmark, and by the Ministry of Economic Affairs and Communications in Estonia! It further accentuates the difficulty of setting up cooperation, particularly multilateral cooperation. However, some countries having the same level of maturity and organization, or close relationships will cooperate more easily. Another reason is that cooperation requires states to share their information and processes, to which they are reluctant. This is one of the reasons why cooperation in this area is mainly for defensive purposes and is not very proactive.

Police cooperation has therefore developed along the lines of Europol, which in 2013 created the Europol's European Cybercrime Center (EC3), whose aim is to *"strengthen law enforcement responses to cybercrime in the EU and thus help protect European citizens and businesses"*.

Europol was initially an office created in 1992 by the Treaty of the Union to process intelligence on criminal activities in Europe. It became a European agency by decision of the European Council of Justice and Internal Affairs Council in April 2009. Based at Europol, EC3 complements the activities of ENISA by specializing in the fight against cybercrime that affects economic activities and goes against the values defended by the EU (computer attacks against the banking sector or child pornography activities). Its main missions concern cyber-crimes committed by organized groups, those that seriously affect victims (such as cases of sexual exploitation of minors) and those that may affect critical infrastructures and information systems of the EU. The EC3 implements with ENISA the resources to collaborate with national CERTs and national judicial institutions in order to facilitate the often international and complex criminal investigations.

6.1.4. Complexity of the System

Because of the differences between states in term of cyber security maturity level, laws and regulations, or organization of national cyber threats responses teams, standardizing European response to cyber threats is still in its infancy. The conflict between some States including Germany and the EU concerning the NIS Directive (adopted on July 6, 2016) about the transposition deadline for the member states (May 9, 2018) showed the limit of the system. *"After a period of diplomatic hurdles, the EU representatives agreed to respect national sovereignty in cyber security regulations and measures, while Germany transposed a version of the NIS"* (Samonek, 2020).

Another issue is that some states, such as the UK, Denmark, France, and Germany among others have already developed high-performance teams that have the experience and funds to provide the necessary response to cyber threats to their country. The legitimacy of the ENISA has thus been questioned, as it did not have the power to overcome national policies. One more problem is that even if the EU recognizes cyber threats as a problem that should be addressed at a global level, national security of its members is beyond its jurisdiction. Samonek underlines the risk that only the least advanced countries in terms of cybersecurity will be interested in a common force, and that the most advanced will be reluctant to share their expertise. According to this author, it would be more relevant to develop a mutual assistance platform between national cyber security agencies, and to play a mediating and advising role, rather than trying to override the security sovereignty of states.

Besides potential rivalries and perceptions of cybersecurity, another question has to be raised: EU is perfectly capable of coordinating a military response in case of conflict, because the notion of conflict has been well defined. However, the perimeter of cyber warfare is not that explicit, nor are the rules of engagement. *"Whether a cyber-attack can be considered an armed attack [...], depends on its consequences rather than the instruments used"* (Latici, 2020).

This does not help define the concept of cyber warfare. Attacks may come from Russia and target French companies, but it does not mean that Russia is attacking France. The distinction between private and public interests could be made, but if a large private telecom operator is targeted, the consequences of this attack have Europe-wide repercussions, potentially also at the military level that could use the networks of this operator. And in other cases, Russian intelligence is directly suspected, as it was the case in 2021 with a hack on several Centreon servers discovered by the ANSSI that found *"several similarities with previous campaigns attributed to the intrusion set named Sandworm"* (France 24, 02/16/21).

On April 27, 2007, the first cyber-attack targeting a state structure took place in Estonia. This large-scale attack against the infrastructure of a state was attributed to Russia by the Estonian authorities from the very beginning. Russia would have used botnets to increase the number of computers involved in the denial-of-service attack against Estonia, contributing directly to this attack. Even if the evidence for such a claim is lacking, it alerted the States to the reality of these new threats, and on the urgent need to focus on harmonizing a common response, which can only be achieved through strong coordination.

6.2. Cyber Defense Strategies in the United States

6.2.1. DoD's Authority to take the Lead

Early in 2017, the importance of cyber defense was made clear by a White House direction that United States Cyber Command be elevated to the status of a Unified Combatant Command focused on cyberspace operations (Garamone, 2017)). In issuing this Command the President stated: *"The elevation of United States Cyber Command demonstrates our increased resolve against cyberspace threats and will help reassure our allies and partners and deter our own adversaries"* (Matishak, p. 1).

As discussed in prior chapters, on the domestic front in the United States, it is the Department of Homeland Security's responsibility to lead and coordinate, the nation's defense. Most national governments have a governance structure that requires certain agencies to take the lead based on criteria including the sector involved, the severity of the attack, and attribution to the attacker (Greiman, 2021). In the United States, the Department of Defense DoD) takes the lead only on the most serious cases – about the top 2% of attacks with responsibility at the Department of Homeland Security (DHS), the Treasury Department, or the sector specific lead agency for the other 98% of the attacks (Treasury, 2019). Pre-decisional operational plans will be in place unless and until a new administration issues new Executive Orders or policy directive that may change prior operational plans. Thus, the definition and criteria for resilience is constantly evolving based on changing administrations, government policies and world events. In Presidential Policy Directive 20 (PPD- 20), the United States government is required to *"conduct all cyber operations consistent with the U.S. Constitution and other applicable laws and policies of the United States, including Presidential orders and directives"* (PPD-20, 2012). Under the Directive, *"special Presidential approval is required for any cyber operations – including cyber collection"* (p. 9, IV).

6.2.2.   U.S. Department of Defense Resilience Strategy

United States military strategy defines cyber resilience as a multifaceted operation. In its 2018 National Defense Strategy it set the following major goals: (1) Defending the Homeland from Attack; (2) Sustaining Joint Force military advantages, both globally and in key regions; (3) Prioritize investments in cyber defense, resilience, and the continued integration of cyber capabilities into the full spectrum of military operation; (4) Build a more lethal force; and (5) Build and maintain robust international alliances and partnerships to deter shared threats and increase international security and stability (DoD, 2018b).

DOD cannot, however, foster resilience in organizations that fall outside of its authority. In order for resilience to succeed as a factor in effective deterrence, other agencies of the government must work with critical infrastructure owners and operators and the private sector more broadly to develop resilient and redundant systems that can withstand a potential attack. Effective resilience measures can help convince potential adversaries of the futility of commencing cyberattacks on U.S. networks and systems. Improving cooperation to manage systemic cyber risk in an evolving global environment and strengthening public-private international cooperation to protect and build resilience in critical infrastructure is a major objective of the strategy (DoD, 2018a, pp. 10-11).

As the U.S. Department of Defense recognizes in its 2018 National Strategy, States are the principal actors on the global stage, but non-state actors also threaten the security environment with increasingly sophisticated capabilities. Terrorists, trans-national criminal organizations, cyber hackers, and other malicious non-state actors have transformed global affairs with increased capabilities of mass disruption. There is a positive side to this as well, as our partners in sustaining security are also more than just nation-states: multilateral organizations, non-governmental organizations, corporations, and strategic influencers provide opportunities for collaboration and   partnership. Terrorism remains a persistent condition driven by ideology and unstable political and economic structures, despite the defeat of ISIS's physical caliphate (DoD, 2018b).

As described in the 2018 Department of Defense Cyber Strategy, the pursuit of security in cyberspace requires a whole-of-government and international approach due to the number and variety of stakeholders in the domain, the flow of information across international borders, and the distribution of responsibilities, authorities, and capabilities across governments and the private sector. The Department will conduct cyberspace operations to collect intelligence and prepare military cyber capabilities to be used in the event of crisis or conflict. The Department will defend forward to disrupt or halt malicious cyber activity at its source, including activity that falls below the level of armed conflict, and will strengthen the security and resilience of networks and systems that contribute to current and future U.S. military advantages. During wartime, U.S. cyber forces will be prepared to operate alongside air, land, sea, and space forces to target adversary weaknesses, offset adversary strengths, and amplify the effectiveness of other elements of the Joint Force. (DoD, 2018a).

It is argued that the development of defense mechanisms by the U.S. military is still insufficient regarding means and ways, especially in terms of military theory. (DoD, 2020). The U.S. Army Cyberspace Operations Guide uses the term resilience 11 times without defining the meaning of resilience though it does define the terms "measure of performance" and "measure of effectiveness" to describe criteria for cyber measure of effectiveness (MOE) — A criterion used to assess changes in system behavior, capability, or operational environment that is tied to measuring the attainment of an end state, achievement of an objective, or creation of an effect. Measure of performance (MOP) is defined as a criterion used to assess friendly actions that is tied to measuring task accomplishment. (DoD, 2020).

6.2.3.   *Resilience and Operational Excellence*

To address operational excellence in the DoD, the Department initiated the DoD Cybersecurity Culture and Compliance Initiative (DC3I) in 2015 to establish five operational principles – integrity, level of knowledge, procedural compliance, formality and backup and a questioning attitude. Because these principles are fundamental to the DoD cyber enterprise, a systems approach has been taken to implement these principles through education and training, scheduled and spot inspections, periodic and episodic reporting and targeted investment that embraces mission-driven cybersecurity (DoD, 2015). For example, mission assurance in the Department of Defense focuses on the protection, continued function, and resilience of capabilities and assets critical to supporting MEFs, rather than the operational execution of DoD missions themselves (HDGS, 2015). The integration of privacy and civil liberties protections into the Department's cybersecurity activities is also fundamental to safeguarding and securing cyberspace and ensuring resiliency (DoD, 2020).

6.2.4.   *Resilience as it relates to Armed Conflict: Cyber-attack as an Act of War*

Reflecting on the distinctive history of conduct in war, one Chairman of the Joint Chiefs of Staff observed that *"[t]he laws of war have a peculiarly American cast"* (DoD, 2016). And it is also true that the laws of war have shaped the U.S. Armed Forces as much as they have shaped any other armed force in the world (DoD, 2016). Presently, the U.S. position on terms such as the use of force and armed attack has been largely memorialized in the DoD Law of War Manual in section 16. The Manual generally identifies and describes the international legal architecture applied to military cyber activity. However, the Manual also acknowledges that the law of war rules are not framed in terms of specific technological means, and not well settled on precisely how they apply to cyber operations (DoD, 2016). Nonetheless, the law of war affirmatively anticipates technological innovation and contemplates that its existing rules will apply to such innovation, including cyber operations (Koh, 2012). Once again, demonstrating that terminology, in this case, legal terminology is not tethered to a strategic (policy and pre-policy) level understanding of the larger operational environment and norms and practices as elements of national power.

As described by James R. Clapper, former Director of National Intelligence, to the Senate Armed Services Committee on 5 January 2016, as of late 2016 more than 30 nations are developing offensive cyber-attack capabilities (NSA, 2017). The proliferation of cyber capabilities coupled with new warfighting technologies will increase the incidence of standoff and remote operations, especially in the initial phases of conflict. Russia officials, for example, have noted publicly that initial attacks in future wars might be made through information networks in order to destroy critically important infrastructure, undermine an enemy's political will, and disrupt military command and control (Senate, 2017). Most cyber-attacks do not amount to an act of war as defined under international law; nonetheless, serious damage may be incurred including loss of life. As globalization, terrorism, and technological advances continue to impact the means and nature of warfare, clear rules are needed to face imminent threats and to protect against potential serious life-threatening losses.

It is argued that the development of defense mechanisms by the U.S. military is still insufficient regarding means and ways, especially in terms of military theory. (Commin, G. and Filiol, 2015). Since the private sector owns and operates over ninety percent of all of the networks and infrastructure of cyberspace it is thus the first line of defense and demands a need for a uniform cyber resilience strategy in the private sector.

6.2.5. State Practice in the Cyber Domain

State practice in the cyber domain is likely to remain relatively veiled in comparison with the other war fighting domains of – land, air, sea, and space. This impedes the development of customary norms of acceptable and unacceptable behavior through actual state practice. As a result, experts, the public, and Congress alike fear that deterrence is not being well served by generalities. Without definition as to disruptive cyber-attacks and even more so for "destructive" ones – a distinction recognized in the 2014 defense quadrennial review – below the significant consequence threshold, which is not defined. Meanwhile, modern warfare is evolving rapidly, leading to increasingly contested battlespace in the air, sea, and space domains – as well as cyberspace in which our forces enjoyed dominance in our most recent conflicts (DHS, 2014). At the same time, the technology-enabled 21st century operational environment offers new tools for state and non-state adversaries such as terrorists to pursue asymmetric approaches, exploiting where we are weakest. In the coming years, countries such as China will continue seeking to counter U.S. strengths using anti-access and area-denial (A2/AD) approaches and by employing other new cyber and space control technologies (DQR, 2014). Deterring and defeating cyber threats requires a strong, multi-stakeholder coalition that enables the lawful application of the authorities, responsibilities, and capabilities resident across the U.S. Government, industry, and international allies and partners (DQR, 2014).

6.2.6. Resilience and Attribution

Identifying the perpetrator of a cyber-attack can be a challenge, but it is also critical to making decisions about the appropriate response. All countries face a wide range of potential cyber-attackers: cyber terrorists, cyber spies, cyber thieves, cyber hacktivists, and quasi state agents known as cyber warriors (Hollis, 2011; Fischer, et al., 2014). Responding to a cyber-attack requires knowing which individual, state, or organization was behind the attack. Attribution can be complicated by a host of analytical shortcomings, such as those evident in prior intelligence failures, including the flawed estimate of Iraq's weapons of mass destruction program (Erwin, 2013). As previously noted, the sheer number of possible adversaries, from Eastern European hackers to Iranian state-sponsored cyber specialists, makes immediate attribution more difficult. The problems of attribution are illustrated by a recent cyber-attack causing massive damage on a global scale. On December 13, 2020, the United States Cybersecurity and Infrastructure Security Agency (CISA) issued its fifth-ever emergency directive, which mandated government users disconnect from its monitoring service, SolarWinds Orion due to the determination that an "outside nation state" had found a back door into some updated versions of the software (CISA, 2020). Widely believed to be Russian backed hackers it was described by Microsoft's President, Brad Smith as Washington's worst cyberespionage failure on record impacting private companies and governments across the globe calling for more collaborative leadership by the government and the tech sector in the United States. Though no formal attribution has been issued to date, the attack continues to raise serious concerns on the regulation of cyber-attacks and cyber attribution as well as the bringing of these international criminals to justice.

To ensure compliance with international law, any response to a cyber-attack must be consonant with the principles of proportionality. The elimination of signature strikes as part of the armed drone campaign seems to address this issue—between 258 and 307 civilians have been killed in Pakistan alone—and answers critics who claim that drone attacks as a component of cyber warfare have become an extremely useful recruit.

Moreover, attribution of cyber control for article 2 purposes of the Law of War ranging from the Cold War to low intensity conflicts remains a question of fact and law. U.S. national technical means increasingly provide the answer, but not necessarily in real time (DoD, 2016). The battlefield for the cyber domain is vast in comparison to the domains of land, sea, air, and space. It is more malleable, asymmetrical with a far more complex terrain and far mor challenging to prosecute. The choices for response in the cyber domain are more extensive and identifying the attacker far more difficult.

6.3. Summary

This chapter highlighted the role of cyber resilience in national cyber defense in Europe and the United States. Because of the differences between states in term of cyber security maturity level, laws and regulations, or organization of national cyber threats responses teams, standardizing the European response to cyber threats is still in its infancy. In contrast, in the United States military strategy defines cyber resilience as a multifaceted operation. In its 2018 National Defense Strategy it set the following major goals: (1) Defending the Homeland from Attack; (2) Sustaining Joint Force military advantages, both globally and in key regions; (3) Prioritizing investments in cyber defense, resilience, and the continued integration of cyber capabilities into the full spectrum of military operation.

Cyber Resilience: A Global Challenge

Though the National Defense Strategy prioritizes cyber resilience as a major goal it has not yet defined its mission at the operational level. The role of cyber resilience in military cyber strategy remains an urgent matter.

Chapter 7

Organizations and Cyber Resilience

Data stored in a firm would be easier to protect if they would just "stay still" and not be connected to the Internet

Pearlson et al, 2015

This quote reflects well the impossibility of securing data at 100%. All the new technologies developed in recent years only reinforce this impossibility. Companies have opened up access to their systems to their partners, suppliers, and customers, thus making a large amount of data circulate. Factory robotization, task automation and IoT further increases the amount of this data and makes all the departments of a company and its partners interdependent. This data is all the more vulnerable as not all players in the chain will have the same level of security. A flaw in one of the systems puts the entire activity of the organization at risk, from production to delivery and invoicing, among others.

7.1. Organizations and Cyber Security

This digitalization has seen an even greater surge over the past few months with the COVID-19 pandemic. Many companies have been forced to let their employees work remotely, thus going beyond their usual work environment. Because of a lack of time and preparation, most of these employees have not been trained in IT security, and their laptop is often not equipped with antivirus software or VPNs that are sufficiently resistant. Ensuring security when employees work remotely, particularly for companies which were not accustomed to it, is quite a challenge. This is not about to change, with 40% of respondents to an American study saying they prefer to work at home. Weaknesses revealed by the sanitary situation have given cyber criminals an even bigger field to prey on. Today, many studies claim that 80% of European companies have experienced at least one cybersecurity incident in the past year, most of them having detected between one and three attacks in the last 12 months. In 2020, in France alone, cyber-attacks have been multiplied by four compared to 2019. The average cost of these attacks ranged from 101,000 euros for France to 906,000 euros for Germany (Statista, 2021).

Yet, according to a study conducted by IBM and the Ponemon Institute in France, 80% of companies do not have a cyber security incident response plan worthy of the name. Twenty-four percent have one but only partially implemented in the company, 31% have one but very informal and 25% simply do not have one! Furthermore, among those who have a plan, only 8% test and evaluate it quarterly, 8% twice a year and 37% only once a year. Forty-eight percent of companies with a cyber security incident response plan apparently do not have the time or processes to evaluate and update it (Ponemon, 2017).

However, large companies now consider that the question is not if they will have to suffer a cyber-attack, but when, and 56% of them think that cyber security has become a priority issue. For instance, 50% of French companies stated having a cybersecurity strategy in 2018 and have spent about 3 million euros in 2020 to strengthen their security systems.

Yet, the paradox is that the more companies seek to improve their level of cyber security, the more they increase the number of entities that will intervene on their system, making them even more at risk. Indeed, they have more and more relationships with system integrators and external service providers on which they rely for many of their applications. These providers are supposed to ensure a high level of security when developing a system and integrating company data, but it is not always the case. As stated by cyber security specialists, even a provider who is certified in cyber security will not be able to provide a 100% secure application. Moreover, companies also interact with a lot of different suppliers and customers, thus offering as many access doors as possible in their systems. Figure 7.1 represents the complexity of the relationships and the resulting opacity.

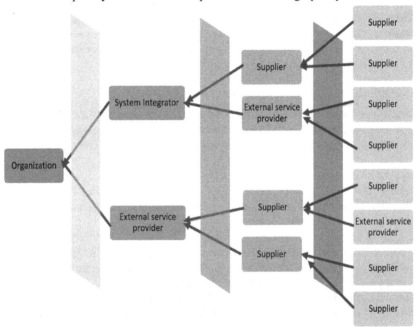

Figure 7.1: *Opacity of the relationships*

(Source: National Institute for Standards and Technology)

The risk related to a third-party is not often taken into account in business decisions. An expert in cyber security for a large firm in Europe related the bad experience he had with one of their service providers. After auditing a provider, which itself had its cyber security level certified by an independent agency, the security expert discovered a potentially dangerous weakness. He alerted the head of the IS department, which in turn contacted the department using the system. The response given by the department shows the level of ignorance of cyber risks: "*If they are certified, everything is fine, and in any case, it is up to them to assume the technical risks, not us".* For many companies, cyber security is still a technician's thing, decoupled from operational activity. Furthermore, cyber security is seen as a cost, and the money invested is supposed to ensure security. Certifications are a guarantee of quality, but once again, they reflect many realities, with auditors' skills varying widely. As an example, a security expert from a mid-sized company, while trying to verify an auditor's skills, managed to hack the certification agency's systems in 30 minutes. Still, companies will be seeking program certification and frameworks to rely on, whether they are specifically dedicated to cyber security or not. As another example, COBIT 5 (Control Objectives for Information and related Technology), initiated by ISACA, was specifically designed to take charge of IT risk management and control investments. It tends to become a unifying tool for the governance of information systems by progressively integrating the contributions of other standards such as ITIL or ISO 9000.

The framework for Cobit in Table 7.1 proposes an evaluation system on 34 IT-related processes established in 4 areas including: planning and organization, acquisition and deployment, supply and support, and supervision.

Table 7.1: *COBIT 5 evaluation system*

Planning & Organization	11 objectives cover everything concerning strategy and tactics. They identify the means enabling IT to contribute most effectively to the achievement of the company's business objectives.
Acquisition & Deployment	6 objectives cover the implementation of IT strategy, identification, acquisition, development, installation of IT solutions and their integration into business processes.
Supply & Support	13 objectives cover the delivery of the required IT services (operations, security, emergency plans and training).
Supervision:	4 objectives enable management to assess the quality and compliance of IT processes with control requirements.

The model is a framework for the enterprise governance of information and technology and not specifically on cyber security. However, it offers a good overview of the systems and through quality control can be a good start. Seeking to manage risks is a first step towards security, the second step being the implementation of a cyber security policy.

As data privacy requirements become stricter across all states in the U.S. and in Europe, companies have to show they are taking it seriously. They are therefore turning to certifications that enable them to carry out an audit of their cybersecurity, but also to prove to their customers and various stakeholders that they have done everything possible to protect their data. Used by at least a third of organizations, ISO 27001 outlined in Table 7.2 is the international standard that describes best practice for implementing an information security management system. It is an ISO 9000-based approach (Plan / Do / Check / Act).

Table 7.2: *ISO 27001 overview*

Plan: Setting objectives and action plans	Identification of assets
	Risk analysis
	Selecting the WSIS perimeter
Do: Implementation and operation of the measures and the policy	Establish a risk management plan
	Deploy security measures
	Train and educate staff
	Detect incidents continuously to react quickly
Check: Measure the results of the actions implemented.	Internal audits of WSIS compliance and effectiveness
	Review the adequacy of the ISS policy with its environment
	Monitor the effectiveness of the measures and the compliance of the system
	Monitor residual risks
Act: Implementation and follow-up	Plan and monitor corrective and preventive action.

Following this standard has advantages on four levels. It allows for identification of the measures to be put in place, to regularly ensure their effectiveness, to better control risks, and finally to improve the confidence of associates, partners, and customers. It is also an international reference that facilitates exchanges. The limit of this norm is that it does not impose a minimum level of security to be achieved.

To better control their level of security, organizations can use frameworks developed by associations or government authorities to help businesses protect themselves.

The National Institute of Standards and Technology (NIST) proposes a framework (updated in 2018) that is complex enough for universities to offer training to be able to apply it (NIST, 2018). This framework, that includes 108 Subcategories, was developed to assist organizations in becoming proactive about managing their information systems security risk. The objective is to minimize the likelihood of breaches and establish a resilient cybersecurity infrastructure. It consists of three parts, *Core*, *Implementation Tiers* and *Profile*.

The NIST cybersecurity framework Core is built on five pillars that are summarized in Figure 7.2.

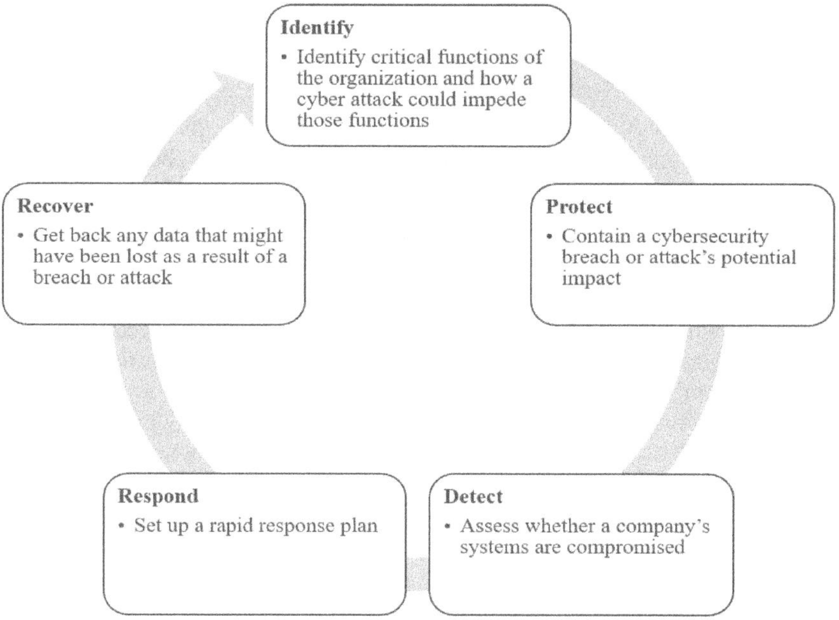

Figure 7.2: *NIST Cybersecurity Framework, An Iterative Perspective*

Applying this framework is an ongoing effort, as the cyber infrastructure and relationships between a company's stakeholders will always be evolving. As any risk analysis and management plan, these five steps must be performed on a regular basis.

1. *Identify*

The first step is to identify the critical functions of the organization, and how a cyber-attack could affect them. For example, if the company performs automatic restocking for its customers, any attack on its SRM (Supplier Relationship Management) system would block production and sales.

It is also important for the organization to identify the weaknesses of its stakeholders, which by the effect of chaining could compromise it, as you are never as strong as your weakest link. The NIST recommends identifying the business environment the organization supports including the organization's role in the supply chain.

2. *Protect*

The Protect Function supports "*the ability to limit or contain the impact of a potential cybersecurity event*". This includes everything the company is going to do to protect itself, at the infrastructure, systems and human levels. For instance, it will include the policy put in place for password management and data access, user training, regular maintenance among other functions.

3. *Detect*

The Detect Function defines "*the appropriate activities to identify the occurrence of a cybersecurity event*". It focuses on the capacity of the organization to detect anomalies and events, as well as their potential impact. It helps organizations to implement security continuous monitoring capabilities and to maintain detection processes.

4. *Respond*

This function helps identify "*appropriate activities to take action regarding a detected cybersecurity incident*". It concerns technical intervention, but also coordination with all stakeholders, including law enforcement agencies. It also includes mitigation activities that could be performed to prevent the event from expanding, forensic analysis, and assessment of the impact of incidents.

5. *Recover*

The Recover Function identifies "*appropriate activities to maintain plans for resilience and to restore any capabilities or services that were impaired due to a cybersecurity incident*". The objective is to get back any data that might have been lost as a result of a breach or attack. Working on processes and procedures to restore systems and/or assets affected by an attack is the first step to a cyber resilience plan.

In order for organizations to evaluate the degree to which an organization's cybersecurity program exhibits the characteristics of their framework, another element of the framework can be used, *Implementation Tiers*. The objective of this element is to help stakeholders understand how their organization compares to its peers and see where improvements are needed. It describes the degree to which an organization's cybersecurity risk management practices conforms to the characteristics defined in the Framework. Still, it should not be considered as a maturity framework, but as a scoring model. The main objective here is to manage risks as shown in Figure 7.3.

Table 7.3: *Summary of tiers – NIST framework*

Tier 1: Partial	Security awareness very limited; no specific training; risk management implemented irregularly on a case-by-case basis; organization is unaware of the cyber risks in their supply chain
Tier 2: Risk-Informed	Awareness of cybersecurity risks; employees and cybersecurity professionals have received specific training; cyber risk assessment of organizations assets occurs but not regularly.
Tier 3: Repeatable	Cybersecurity professionals possess necessary skills and knowledge to perform their roles; employees receive regular training and information; processes are defined, implemented, and reviewed on a regular basis.
Tier 4: Adaptive	Cybersecurity professionals are reactive and proactive. Managers integrate cyber risk in their risk management; cybersecurity risk is integrated into the organizational culture; organization understands cyber risks in supply chain and uses real-time information to regularly act against those risks

The last element of the NIST framework is the Profiles. Once an organization has reviewed all the categories and subcategories of the framework, it can identify its profiles and how it can improve its cybersecurity posture. Profiles are primarily used to identify and prioritize opportunities for improving cybersecurity at an organization. They can also be used to communicate within an organization or between organizations.

These implementation frameworks are useful for businesses and have enabled large companies to achieve a satisfactory level of cyber security. However, they also sometimes confer a false sense of security. Despite a record number of attacks in recent years, corporate security managers are quite confident in their ability to respond to an attack. This optimistic bias is generally shared by executives, who, although more of them are nowadays briefed on cyber security issues, are not experts and have difficulty understanding the issues in detail. They believe they have recruited the right people to manage cyber risks. Increasing budgets for managing these risks reinforces this sense of security. Moreover, tech people focus more on preventing attacks and how systems can recover than on how a business can carry on after losing its data. Yet, a cybersecurity program cannot substitute for cyber resilience.

Today, most of the companies are aware of the cyber risks. Many of them have reinforced their security and now turn to the second step: focus on the consequences when cyber criminals still manage to penetrate their systems. Companies need to extend their cyber risk management focus to the potential impact they could have on their reputation and customers and recognize the unplanned business consequences from activity in cyberspace. This awareness is the first step towards building cyber resilience for businesses, which we will discuss in the next section. This means be willing to share information with partners both in the private sector and at the governmental level.

7.2.   Organizations and Cyber Resilience

Cyber resilience is not commonly developed in companies, even those having a high level of security level. Sometimes being certified, following ISO 270001 recommendations gives a false sense of security. These analysis frameworks address the issue of cyber resilience but at a too general level, and do not provide a precise roadmap for any company wishing to put in place a good cyber resilience policy. The result is that many companies believe that they can ensure cyber resiliency by simply following the NIST or other experts' framework recommendations.

However, while security remains a key factor in the concept of cyber resilience, it is now an integral part of a more global approach involving strategy, crisis management and business continuity, among other things. It is still not common practice. As a study conducted in France in 2017 on the importance of cyber resilience for effective security shows, only a few organizations have a high degree of cyber resilience, and 73% believe that their organization is not prepared to recover from a cyber-attack (Ponemon Institute, 2017). Half of them are good at detection, prevention, and containment, but only 27% consider they are good at recovery.

According to the study, it is the lack of organization and risk awareness that is most detrimental to cyber-resilience. Sixty-eight percent of respondents said that lack of organization and preparedness was the biggest barrier, and 52% said lack of risk awareness, analysis and evaluation prevented organizations from building optimal e-resilience. The complexity of the company's procedures is also perceived as an obstacle by 47% of those questioned. Another result shows that 70% of respondents consider that the incidents they experienced involved human error.

7.2.1. Supply Chain Resiliency

One of the major cyber risks is undeniably the complexity of the supply chain. It is almost impossible to know how its Tier 3 or 4 suppliers ensure the security of their own systems. Yet, a weakness in one of them can be traced back to the company's data. Even without reaching that end, and without data theft, a supplier who loses data or has their production system hacked will not be able to deliver on time, which will impact the customer's business operations. The chaining effect of a cyber-attack on one of a companies' suppliers can stop their business. Supply chain resiliency has been defined as "*the ability of the supply chain to cope with unexpected disturbances*" (Christopher, 2011). One of its characteristics is a business-wide recognition of where the supply chain is most vulnerable. To show the significance of supply chain cyber risk, the supply chain risk Management Category has been added to the Framework Core in the NIST standards (NIST 1.1, 2018). However, they focus only on cyber security aspects.

The complexity and opacity of the supply chain network means that most companies do not have a global vision of their supply chain and are therefore unable, beyond the risky entry points, to identify the consequences of a cyber-attack on the entire chain and the systems to be bypassed or put back into operation as a priority to restore activity as quickly as possible. The phenomenon has been noted by the National Institute for Standards and Technology that identified "*how the diverse types of relationships between these different categories of actors*" can "*affect an organization's visibility*", preventing it from controlling its supply chain.

To be able to do so, companies would have to map their supply chain, which can be complicated considering the number of suppliers a company may have, and their willingness to share the type of information necessary to understand the overall process. As the supply chain could be the first impacted by a cyber-attack, and the most vulnerable because of the number of suppliers and partners, its design, and business continuity all have a role to play in creating resilience (Waters, 2011).

7.2.2. Cyber resilience framework for companies

As discussed so far, an organization's ability to be cyber resilient will initially depend on its level of maturity in cyber security. It makes sense, as "*most cyber resilience measures assume leverage, or enhance a variety of cyber security measures. Cyber security and cyber resiliency measures are most effective when applied together in a balanced way*" (MITRE, 2015), as "*the cyber resiliency goals of anticipate, withstand, recover, and adapt complement the security objectives of confidentiality, integrity, and availability that are conventional goals of systems security engineering*".

Cyber resiliency requires a good understanding of cyber risks and their impact at every level of the organization. Frameworks developed by government or certification authorities show that mobilizing all stakeholders is essential to ensure not only cyber security, but also crisis response and business continuity. In order to identify these risks and their potential consequences, the International Risk Governance Council (IRGC) has developed a framework that helps identify which stakeholders should be involved in risk management, based on the dominant characteristic of the problem domain: simplicity, complexity, uncertainty, or ambiguity (MITRE, 2015). Applying this framework to cyber resilience helps to identify when we leave the domain of cyber security to enter the domain of cyber resilience. Indeed, as long as the risk is simple, it is usually clearly identified. It is therefore possible to put routines in place to limit or even avoid it. As soon as it becomes more complex, it can be essential to mobilize external experts to better understand it, but it is still possible to anticipate it. That is still part of a classical cyber security management approach.

When the level of risk becomes more difficult to estimate, and the level of uncertainty is high, it seems more appropriate to involve experts and all stakeholders potentially concerned. According to the IRGC, these risks require *"reflective discourses with agency staff and experts as well as stakeholders in order to find the best compromise between too much and too little precaution when facing uncertain outcomes"* (IRGC, 2020, p.06). Their definition of a risk ambiguity is that a risk is ambiguous when there are *"different interpretations of the information available, which leads to divergent perspectives on the risk, including the likelihood and severity of potential adverse outcomes"*. Identifying and discussing the nature and importance of these risks will require help from a wide range of stakeholders. This notion of ambiguous risk is totally transposable to cyber resilience, as the potential impact of an attack remains difficult to identify and measure, since the number of stakeholders involved can be significant due to the chaining effect.

Uncertainty and ambiguity are not easy to control. As the question is how best to respond when the problem arises, it is more about cyber resilience than cyber security. The risk management escalator is shown in Figure 7.3.

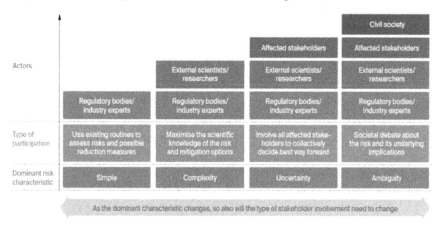

Figure 7.3: *IRGC - the risk management escalator*

The value of this framework is that it demonstrates the importance of involving all stakeholders. It is therefore a good way to approach cyber resilience. It is indeed not easy for organizations to start thinking about their cyber resilience. Often relying on cyber security principles, they forget the essential elements such as their external environment, their employees, and their interactions.

7.3. Rethinking Cyber Resilience

Starting to think about implementing cyber resilience will require companies to ask themselves the right questions. To this end, the set of questions (known as the "Heilmeier Catechism") developed by George H. Heilmeier, a former DARPA director (1975-1977), can be used as a "preflight checklist," which "*provides a routine for safely and successfully launching a research projec*t" (Shapiro, 1994). The Heilmeier Catechism is an important evaluation tool as we face the challenges of integration and global interconnectedness of an ever-expanding cyberspace. Table 7.4 highlights the interest of rethinking resilience utilizing the questions raised in the Heilmeier Catechism as a starting point for achieving success in the development of frameworks and standards for cyber resilience.

Table 7.4: *The Heilmeier Catechism*

The Heilmeier Catechism	Rethinking Resilience to Achieve Success
What are you trying to do? Articulate your objectives using absolutely no jargon.	Think not only about your objectives, but how you can lift the constraints that will impede reaching those objectives
How is it done today, and what are the limits of current practice	Think not only about the limits of current practice, but also about the opportunities for improving the organization, building resource capacity, and changing the culture
What is new in your approach and why do you think it will be successful?	Think about moving away from a reactionary approach to events to one of strategic prioritization and investment
Who cares? If you are successful, what difference will it make?	Think not only about the difference it will make within your organization, but how you can improve life for everyone across the digital divide
What are the risks and the pay-offs?	Think not only about the risks, but about the opportunities for creating a safer cyber world
How much will it cost?	Think not only about the cost of development, but the long term benefits the change will bring
How long will it take?	Think not only about the time it will take, but the resources and knowledge you can develop for long term sustainability
What are the measures of success?	Think not only about the key environmental factors in achieving success, but the meaning of success to the organization and the outside world

7.4. Summary

Answering these questions will be a first step towards a more strategic vision of cyber resilience. Indeed, what will be important besides its capacity to counter cyber-attacks is the capacity of an organization to learn from what happened. The idea is also to think about what better cyber resilience can do, not only for the organization, but also for its environment.

As we have seen so far, an organization's ability to be cyber resilient will initially depend on its level of maturity in cyber security. However, frameworks developed by government or certification authorities show that mobilizing all stakeholders is essential to ensure not only cyber security, but also crisis response and business continuity. A good level of cyber resilience will depend on a multitude of technological and human factors. While the technical aspects can be covered by cyber security professionals, the first step towards cyber resilience is to build "cyber awareness". This cyber awareness cannot be achieved overnight and must be built carefully and continuously. To do so, it is relevant to adopt a multi-criteria approach that will allow cyber resilience to be embedded in the organization's culture.

Chapter 8

Developing a Multi-criteria Cyber Resilience Framework for Organizations

A cyber resilient culture is a state of maturity in which all staff make conscious efforts to behave in ways that protect the organization against cyber threats; and in which they are supported by appropriate mechanisms to inculcate the required behavioral changes

Oliver Wyman

In this chapter we propose a new framework for cyber resilience represented by the following four domains:

- Organize for Cyber Resilience
- Develop a Cyber Resilient Leadership Team
- Regulate Cyber Resilience
- Connect with Stakeholders to Build Resilience

Most of the research has been focused on operational aspects of cyber resilience. A company that would decide to implement a cyber resilience plan is going to look to recognized models to apply. This can be, for example, the MITRE framework, which includes over 200 metrics. These metrics are intended to assess an already implemented cyber resilience policy, and even if companies wanted to use them to implement a good policy, it would be hard for non-experts to distinguish between the must-have metrics and the not-so-must-have ones. Moreover, implementing strong policies will not be effective if no one applies them, whether through ignorance, lack of conviction or lack of skills. A small cyber resilience plan will be more effective if it is understood, integrated and manageable by everyone than a complex plan that can only be understood by IS experts. The organizational and human aspects are therefore crucial and will require a change in both strategy and behavior.

8.1. A Framework for Cyber Resilience

In this respect, ensuring cyber resilience awareness leading to a change in behavior is similar to implementing a Corporate and Social Responsibility (CSR) policy. To be effective, CSR must be taken into account in all daily activities, as well as in strategic decisions, which must also be the case for cyber resilience. The literature in this field is a source of inspiration and can serve as a basis for the development of a multi-criteria cyber-resilience framework. One of the most inspiring frameworks is the framework developed by Bertels (2010). It is based on the fact that *"business leaders are starting to recognize that organizational culture plays a fundamental part in the shift toward sustainability"* (Bertels 2010, p.8), but *"lack a clear understanding of how to embed sustainability in their day-to-day decisions and processes"*. The idea is to consider all the elements in the organization likely to foster the emergence and continuity of CSR, and to promote good practices.

Following the same logic of reflection, we have identified the main elements necessary for the implementation of a culture of cyber resilience. Developing a cyber resilience culture requires indeed a strong involvement of the executive team and all employees. The technical aspects are covered by the company's cyber security policies and voluntarily excluded from this reflection. The challenge will therefore be to decompartmentalize the issue of cyber security in order to strengthen resilience, by moving away from a treatment that is too exclusively technical and/or too digital to adopt a multidisciplinary approach to cyber risk management.

Beyond technical aspects, a cyber resilience framework that will become part of the organization's culture must cover different domains: 1) *organizational*, which will address aspects of strategy and governance; 2) *development*, which will address human aspects, particularly in terms of recruitment and training; 3) *regulation*, in order to measure and trace events and thus optimize the response; 4) and finally *connection*, which will take into account the entire network of stakeholders both internal to the company as well as the myriad of external stakeholders including, the supply chain, customers, the regulators, collaborators and industry partners in order to communicate and be transparent in the event of cyber threats and attacks.

These domains are summarized in the framework shown in Figure 8.1.

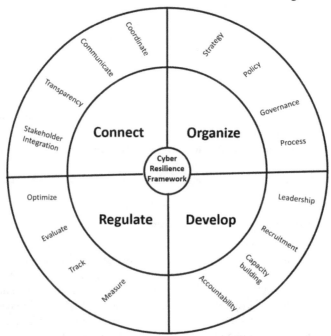

Figure 8.1: *A portfolio approach to embedding cyber resilience*

8.1.1. Organize

Research shows that response and recovery from a cyber-attack and the return to a normative state or reinvention of its operations is not a plan companies can come up with when prevention has failed, but a "*strategy in itself, particularly when dealing with systems that are so complex that it is infeasible to analyze and prevent every way in which the system can fail*" (Estay et al, 2020).

If an organization's ability to be cyber resilient will initially depend on its level of maturity in cyber security, this will still not appear spontaneously. It has to be formalized and integrated into the company's strategy. It is through a shift in perspective on security that organizations can move from cybersecurity to cyber resilience: no longer just seen as a set of preventive measures, it will also offer powerful anticipatory capabilities to stay one step ahead of the consequences of an attack.

The consequence of its inclusion in the strategy is a clearly identified policy and governance, leading to the implementation of well-defined processes that must be continuously updated and evaluated for effectiveness.

1. Strategy

Obtaining a good level of cyber resilience requires first to identify critical digital assets. They can be critical for different reasons: it can be a production tool which, if attacked, would halt the operation of the plant. It can be a customer database which, if attacked, would impact not only these customers but also the reputation of the company. They can be critical because of their level of dependency with other systems. For instance, it can be a system managing supplier relations which, if attacked, would impact all partners. The next step will be to identify the recovery time once the system has been compromised. Is it a matter of hours, days, weeks? Then what would be the impact on customers? On company's finances? Quantifying the impact to the business would be essential if a particular kind of disruption should occur. Once the critical digital assets have been identified, a clear incident response strategy must be defined. The response strategy will identify what should be done to ensure business continuity, and all the stakeholders involved in the response plan.

Technology continues to evolve, as well as business activities, and it makes the cyber threat scenario more volatile than ever. In addition to this, there are staff turnovers, which justifies that this plan has to be regularly updated.

2. Policy

Once the cyber resilience strategy has been defined, existing policies have to be reviewed and new ones developed. This review can start with an internal audit that will help to examine the overall security environment of the company as well as the controls governing individual information systems. Security audits will look at technologies, procedures, documentation, training, and personnel. The result of these audits will help companies and their stakeholders to develop a set of policies that will protect them and be embedded in their daily activities. These new policies will take into account evolution of the technology and its usage by collaborators. For instance, many companies have to adapt their already existing policies to teleworking or IoT.

3. *Governance*

"*Governance is the cyber resilience domain that contains the policies and procedures to manage cyber resilience from a strategic point of view*" (Carías et al, 2020).

A consideration of cyber resilience incorporated into the organization's strategy will require the adaptation of IS governance to system and data security issues. The governance must incorporate strategies for protection, detection and response at an information systems, cyber security, and organization level. It is necessary to set up a crisis management system that can operate in real time. The objective is also to plan the management of the consequences of the attack in its various aspects: human, financial, reputation and responsibilities. During an attack, it is important for the organization to be able to make extremely quick decisions in a very limited time. A good governance will allow identification of who is authorized to make decisions if anything comes up and identify the processes to follow.

4. *Process*

To ensure that cyber resilience is taken into account at every level in the organization, new processes have to be set up. One of them will concern the process of acquiring tools and systems.

According to the MITRE report, "*incorporating cyber resiliency measures into the acquisition process increases the likelihood that the system will continue to provide mission-critical and mission-essential capabilities in spite of adversarial actions and will give cyber defenders the necessary tools to respond quickly and effectively to the adversary*". At the employee level, the implementation of specific processes will force them to respect the measures put in place. For example, they may be required to change their password every six weeks, or they will not be able to connect to the network. This is a cyber security action, but it increases their awareness of the risk of data theft and helps them think about the "what if" scenario.

8.1.2. *Develop*

From a psychological perspective, resilience is the ability to successfully cope with a situation that is highly stressful because of its harmfulness or risk, and to recover, adapt, and succeed in living and developing positively despite these adverse circumstances. In an organizational context, the ability to adapt is perhaps the most important. One way to do this is to keep the organization's primary focus in mind. Take the example of a restaurant that can no longer accommodate customers because of the sanitary situation. Owners may be devastated because they feel compelled to close, while others will keep in mind the purpose of their business: to serve food to their customers. With this goal in mind, they will adapt and organize take-out sales or deliveries. This ability to adapt can only be initiated or maintained through employee awareness of cyber security issues and how a cyber disaster could impact the company. The permanent reflection must be: how will we be impacted and how can we continue the activity? This reflection can only be fed through good leadership, recruitment of the right people and/or training of the entire staff. The predominant concern in this reflection is accountability, at the organization and employees' level.

5. *Leadership*

Cyber resilience is not something we think of spontaneously. You have to know the issues, think about scenarios, the chaining effects of a potential problem and how it would affect all stakeholders. This change in thinking can only be achieved if it is driven by a leader who knows how to systematically ask the right questions to bring others to this reflection. All employees should adopt a cyber resilient mind-set. This requires a focus beyond prevention to adaptation, recovery and reinvention because returning to normalcy may not be possible.

6. *Recruitment*

Many companies do not have a high level of cyber resilience because they lack the expertise at a technical and governance level. Recruiting the right people to implement good cyber security seems therefore obvious. There can be no cyber resilience without cyber security. However, it's not just about building a defense plan. It's also about understanding what's at stake for the company, and therefore understanding its business. This may require different skills. In the same way that IT profiles are different from IS profiles, the cyber resilience expert will not be the same as the cyber security expert. The cyber resilience expert must be able to identify the consequences of possible breaches on the business and prioritize the restart of activities. While large companies can afford to hire such a profile, small and medium-sized companies can call on external experts to support them initially.

7. *Training*

About one-third of cyber-attacks are caused by human negligence. One study found that up to 12,000 laptops are lost each week and up to 600,000 per year at U.S. airports (Ponemon, 2008). Forty-five percent of healthcare security breaches occur on stolen laptops (Santamaria 2016). In France alone, about 10% of managers in medium-sized companies have had their computers stolen (Statista, 2015). On half of the stolen professional laptops, the data was not encrypted. Employees are the biggest vulnerability and hackers know it. They will focus on them to get access to the system.

As the SETA states, it is necessary to "*instill in personnel a desire and a commitment to be proactive in the execution of their security duties*". Employees need to understand the consequences of a security breach and that they are the first line of defense when it comes to threats such as phishing, spear phishing and malware. It is critical to set up security awareness training for employees, contractors, and partners, especially along the supply chain who interact with corporate systems and have access to the company's data.

8. *Accountability*

According to the National Institute of Standards and Technology, accountability is "*the principle that an individual is entrusted to safeguard and control equipment, keying material, and information and is answerable to a proper authority for the loss or misuse of that equipment or information*".

9. *Company accountability*

Companies are responsible for the data they store and use. In Europe, the General Data Protection Regulation (GDPR) has reinforced the responsibility of institutions (public and private). Since May 25, 2018, they have to ensure optimal protection of the data they handle and prove their compliance at all times. To do this they must map their personal data and their processing, set up procedures and train their employees.

Following inspections or complaints, in the event of non-compliance with the requirements of the GDPR or the law on the part of companies, the CNIL's restricted panel may impose sanctions on companies that do not comply with these texts. The GDPR penalty can amount to 20,000,000 euros or 4% of their total worldwide turnover of the previous fiscal year (whichever amount is higher). In 2020, the number of fines for non-compliance with the GDPR amounted to 171 million euros!

From a cyber resilience perspective, it means that companies are also responsible to their partners and shareholders. They must be able to show them a business continuity plan in case of a data breach.

10. *Collaborator accountability*

As companies are responsible for the data and its use, they must rely on their employees to ensure that it is properly managed on a daily basis. The GDPR requires companies to train their employees, but for non-European companies, there is no obligation. These companies must therefore teach their employees to be responsible for the data they handle. From a technical standpoint, the cyber security expert will have accountability and authority to execute cyber security for all information technology and operational technology infrastructure.

From a cyber resilience standpoint, department managers should be responsible for identifying the activities under their control that are priorities in getting the business back on track in case of a threat or disruption.

Once employees have been trained in cyber security, they become responsible for respecting the measures put in place by the company. For example, they will be responsible for the use they make of the equipment provided by the company.

8.1.3. *Regulate.*

The MITRE technical report on Cyber Resiliency Metrics, Measures of Effectiveness, and Scoring provides companies with a reference for IT professionals and managers "*concerned with assessing or scoring cyber resiliency for systems and missions; selecting cyber resiliency metrics to support cyber resiliency assessment; and defining, evaluating, and using cyber resiliency measures of effectiveness for alternative cyber resiliency solutions*". Many tools and directives exist to help companies to measure, track, evaluate and optimize their cyber resilience approach.

1. Measure

To measure a company's cyber resilience to a crisis, it is necessary to assess the processes in place. The IT department must review its relevance to existing cyber threats and test it. It must also be known and controlled. This will require that it be shared with all the stakeholders concerned.

2. Track

Most systems provide detailed traces of their operation (logs, etc.) The major difficulty, which must be anticipated, is to have the tools and skills to analyze these traces.

3. Evaluate

The U.S. Department of Homeland Security created a method enabling organization to self-assess their cyber resilience, using the Cyber Resilience Review (CRR). Conducted by the cyber resilience expert, it is "*an interview-based assessment of an organization's cybersecurity management program. It seeks to understand the cybersecurity management of services, and their associated assets, that are critical for an organization's mission success*" (DHS, 2020). DHS partnered with the CERT Division of the Software Engineering Institute at Carnegie Mellon University to design and deploy the CRR. The concepts of the CRR are derived from the Resilience Management Model (CERT-RMM) developed by Carnegie Mellon University (Carnegie, 2016).

It includes 42 objectives and 141 specific practices from the CERT-RMM, organized into 10 domains. It consists of 299 questions, which may seem excessive and cumbersome for many companies. However, like many methods, it can be used to find the elements that correspond most closely to the processes in place. Moreover, it can be easier for an organization that does not have a high level of maturity in cyber security to use a mission-centric approach and focus on how well cyber resilience objectives are achieved and capabilities provided in the context of the mission, and not include metrics related to vulnerability severity.

Many cyber resiliency metrics can be identified. The US Army Engineer Research and Development Center considers resilience through four domains: physical, information, cognitive, and social. Based on this work, Linkov et al., (2013) have developed a comprehensive framework that can be quite easily applied. They consider that resilience of a cyber system is "*dependent on the effective functioning of all aspects of an organization throughout the event management cycle in the four identified domains*". The metrics should be related to mission or organizational consequences.

Regularly evaluating the ability to resume business after a cyber-attack, beyond checking the capacity of systems to recover, has the advantage of maintaining employee vigilance in this area. It also allows for the systematic integration in the strategic and operational thinking and finally to optimize the processes.

4. Optimize

A regular evaluation of the cyber resilience plan will optimize the performance of the actions implemented. Any evaluation must lead to the re-evaluation of the policies in place, and lead to not only technical but also organizational improvements. This can mean revising the training provided to employees or strengthening critical resources to ensure that the necessary vigilance is maintained on a daily basis.

8.1.4. Connect

"Today's CISO focuses on tier 1 or direct suppliers. Tomorrow's CISO will need to focus on the supply chain"

Chief information security officer (CISO) of a major international bank

As illustrated in the investigation of major cyber-attacks, collective action is essential for resolution of almost all major cyber-attacks. According to the MITRE report, "*cyber resiliency can apply to a system, a system-of-systems, a mission, a business function, an organization, or a cross-organizational mission*".

The recent Solar Winds cyber-attack illustrates the necessity of having a link between the Supply Chain and the organizations they support. The disconnect between units within an organization as illustrated by the Bangladesh Bank Cyberattack between the criminal units and the fraud units is alarming enough, however, in 2013 Target announced that over 40 million credit cards and private data on 70 million customers had been stolen by accessing data on point of sale (POS) systems. And yet, they had implemented security required by the credit card processing requirements. What makes it interesting is that both companies were compliant with their industries standards regulations. It shows that cyber security and resilience cannot be considered in separate silos. The cyber world is vast, and interconnected, so are the risks. One organization can be used as a route to attack another organization in the same supply chain. For a supply chain to work effectively and efficiently, sensitive and confidential information must be shared between many organizations (Davis, 2015). In order to make it work and protect all organizations in the supply chain, all stakeholders should be included in the reflection on cyber security. These stakeholders have to be transparent about their policies of cyber-attacks prevention and communicate anytime something suspicious is detected. Finally, stakeholders who share a system on a daily basis, such as suppliers managing replenishments for their customers, or logistics companies must work together on a coordinated cyber resiliency plan.

1. Integrate stakeholders

Classically, crisis management requirements include all partners and suppliers to be involved in a response plan elaboration. One of the main issues in doing so is that not all stakeholders will have the same level of cyber security or cyber resilience maturity. Therefore, a strategic decision must be made at this level. Should the organization take the risk of working with partners who do not implement the necessary security measures? Should they include this requirement in their contracts with them? Should they invest in supporting their suppliers in implementing better cybersecurity? These questions are not unfamiliar to organizations, insofar as they have already been addressed during the implementation of information systems such as SRM or AOM, for example. Building a cyber resilient supply chain involves identifying processes, integrating the cybersecurity of the chain's stakeholders, and pooling risk management.

2. Be transparent.

The World Economic Forum believes that the issue of cyber resilience must also address issues related to the role of trust, the need for partnerships and the distribution of responsibilities in this matter. A cyber resilience plan developed with all of these stakeholders will identify the responsibilities of each.

Companies must also be transparent to the actors in their chain, and to their customers.

3. Communicate

Transparency also means communicating. Communication will be made at three levels: internally, towards stakeholders and towards customers.

Internal communication is indeed important, as it shows employees how the company reacted in case of a cyber-attack, but also how its system is constantly evolving. It also regularly reminds employees of the challenges of strong cyber security and resilience and the need to integrate it into their daily routine.

Regular communication with stakeholders demonstrates the organization's vigilance and enables the sharing of information, expertise, and best practices.

Finally, communication with customers, especially after a cyber-attack, is crucial. This is consistent with the notion of transparency. In some countries, companies facing a cyber breach have the obligation to inform their customers as soon as possible and be very specific about the stolen data. This is especially important as a direct consequence of a cyber-attack for a company, even if it has demonstrated excellent cyber resilience, will be the lack of trust felt by customers. And the cost of re-acquiring a customer is often higher than the cost of acquiring them! Good communication can help manage this aspect.

4. Coordinate

In the event of a cyber-attack, companies must coordinate their efforts with a large number of actors: law enforcement, external stakeholders and of course their employees. In the same way that cyber security and cyber resilience managers should be identified in an organization, one manager per department or process should also be specifically trained and equipped with tools to react quickly and coordinate with others. It's not when the problem occurs that you have to ask yourself who to turn to. This may sound like basic risk management, but a lot of research has shown that only companies with a high level of risk management maturity know how to coordinate their actions with all stakeholders.

Most companies that have a strong need to control risks seek to develop a risk culture. Each employee will have to take into account the risks inherent to his activity in each process. As soon as it is an element of reporting, it becomes a reflex. The process is the same for cyber resilience. But in the same way that we learn to manage traditional risks, we learn to integrate a vision of cyber resilience.

To make it happen, cyber resiliency needs to be a top priority for the organization, from the board of directors down to every employee. To achieve cyber resiliency, it's important to go beyond establishing a security-conscious culture to fostering a resilient one. By including cyber resilience in the strategy, appointing leaders to implement it, training employees, and finally making it an ongoing process, it will be possible to create this resilience-conscious culture.

8.2. Summary

In this chapter, we have presented a framework that provides a holistic view of cyber resilience. Realizing that building good cyber resilience requires its consideration at all levels of the organization is an important step. Another dimension of cyber resilience that is important to understand is its interconnection with the organization's external environment. Being able to protect one's system and recover in the event of a cyber-attack will do little good if the organization's systems are interconnected with other less protected systems. So cyber resilience is a collective effort. Furthermore, to ensure that it is "practiced" on a daily basis, it must be gradually integrated into the organization's culture, which will require the implementation of well-defined processes and constant communication.

Chapter 9

Catastrophic Potential and the Role of Cyber Resilience

We cannot undo this damage. What is done is done and it will take decades to fix.

John Schindler, former NSA Officer

This quote from former NSA Officer John Schindler highlights the long-term damage that one catastrophic cyber event can generate (NPR, 2015). In this case the extensive losses to millions of citizens from the attack on the U.S. Office of Personnel Management in 2015.

This chapter describes several catastrophic cyber events that highlight the type of threats, the responses under the law, and the impact of the attack. The various approaches taken by nation states emphasizes the importance of defining the scope of cyber responsibility and authority and the appropriateness of retaliatory cyber strikes in a nation's overall defense strategy. The focus in this chapter is on the human response to cyber-attacks and the role that resilience plays in each of these attacks. We use selected cases to apply the Cyber Resilience Framework discussed in the prior chapter to show where a framework might have mitigated or even prevented the attacks that occurred causing serious loss and damage. The case studies include the 2020 Solar Winds attack, the 2015 attack on Ukraine's power grid, the U.S.'s Office of Personnel Management 2015 Data Breach, and the 2014 Sony Pictures Attacks.

One of the greatest threats for catastrophic potential is the Advanced Persistent Threat (APT). A threat actor that possesses sophisticated levels of expertise and significant resources which allow it to create opportunities to achieve its objectives by using multiple threat vectors creates a greater likelihood for catastrophic potential. As defined by NIST's Cyber Lexicon, the advanced persistent threat (APT): (1) pursues its objectives repeatedly over an extended period of time; (2) adapts to defenders' efforts to resist it; and (3) is determined to execute its objectives. Cyber resilience plays a critical role in avoiding catastrophic loss at the strategic, operational, and tactical levels. Based on research studies on Cloud services disruptions, Lloyd's estimates average losses of $53.1 billion, but for an extreme event, they could be as high as US $121.4 billion (Lloyd's, 2017, p. 48). Sources of cyber threats include threats to national security, economic prosperity, critical infrastructure, and civil liberties. Cyber-attacks do not spare any industry and have targeted a diverse group of enterprises. Critical infrastructure in Ukraine has been repeatedly targeted over several years with some utilities switching to manual operation as a defense against cyber-attacks that can use their control networks against them. As most power providers and distributors use outsourced integrators to maintain their networking systems, an attack that causes physical damage could result in weeks of outages while the integrators scramble to replace the physical systems. Additionally, these attacks have spread from the power sector to the oil and natural gas sector in countries like Saudi Arabia. Similar behavior of the malware has been seen targeting and disabling critical safety systems to open the door to potential attacks that could result in physical damage or destruction. Where oil refineries are concerned, if taken to an extreme, the attacks could cause an explosion with loss of life. This scenario could even happen unintentionally, as the attackers are trying to focus on a nearby industrial complex. As shown in Table 9.1, cyber-attacks can have diverse impacts and responses.

Table 9.1: *Major Cyber Events, Impact and Attribution*

Event	Type of Threat	Impact	Attribution
2015 Ukrainian Power Grid	Sabotage and espionage of critical infrastructure	Caused more than 200,000 consumers to lose power.	On October 15, 2020, the U.S. DOJ indicted six members of the Russian military intelligence agency (DOJ, 2020b)
2020 Solar Wind Hack	Espionage-based assault	Broad attack on confidential information of U.S. and UK Government including Homeland Security, the Pentagon, NATO, UK parliament, private industry, and the tech tools used by companies to protect them.	Alleged Russian Hacker Group. No formal attribution to date
2015 U.S. OPM Data Breach	Aggressive Act of Espionage	Data Breach of 21.5 million current and former U.S. government employees	No public attribution due to national security concerns (Finklea et al., 2015).
2014 Sony Pictures Attacks	Critical Infrastructure Cyber-Attack and Economic Crime	US $171M damage, attacked 77 million accounts, described as worse computer data breach in U.S. history	Following the FBI's attribution of the Sony Pictures hack to North Korea on Dec. 19, 2014, the U.S. imposed sanctions against 10 individuals and three entities associated with the country's Pyongyang-based government.

As the evidence reflects, most attacks do not amount to an act of war as defined under international law; because they do not meet the level of force or destruction required. Nonetheless, serious damage may be incurred including loss of life. Based on the significance of critical infrastructure sectors such as energy in the broader national security context, it is in the interest of the federal government to ensure updates to current cyber security regulations to address evolving and emerging threats. To fulfill the federal vision for energy sector security and resilience increasing cooperation between government and energy sector members is likely necessary according to the Idaho National Laboratory (INL, 2016). As globalization, terrorism, and technological advances continue to impact the means and nature of warfare, clear rules are needed to face imminent threats and to protect against potential serious life-threatening losses. The various approaches taken by nation states emphasizes the importance of defining the scope of cyber responsibility and authority and the appropriateness of retaliatory cyber strikes in a nation's overall defense strategy. As an example, the Cyber-attack on the Ukrainian Power Grid was characterized as a test for cyberwar and a political act of aggression, allegedly conducted by the Russians, however, no sanctions were imposed for this act despite the indictment of 6 members of the Russian military agency.

9.1. The Ukrainian Power Grid

On December 23, 2015, the Ukrainian Kyivoblenergo, a regional electricity distribution company, reported service outages to customers. The attack was analyzed by multiple sources including private companies, investigators in Ukraine, and the U.S. government. The analysis revealed many opportunities to stop or prevent this attack which provides many opportunities for improving resilience. A comprehensive investigation concluded the outages were due to a third party's illegal entry into the company's computer and SCADA systems resulting in 225,000 customers to lose power across various areas (E-ISAC, 2016). The remote cyber-attacks directed against Ukraine's electricity infrastructure were described by experts as bold and successful. The cyber operation was highly synchronized, and the adversary was willing to maliciously operate a SCADA system to cause power outages, followed by destructive attacks to disable SCADA and communications to the field. The destructive element is the first time the world has seen this type of attack against OT systems in a nation's critical infrastructure. This is an escalation from past destructive attacks such as (Saudi Aramco and Sony Pictures) that impacted general-purpose computers and servers. Importantly, the investigation revealed that the attack methodology, tactics, techniques, and procedures (TTPs) observed are employable in infrastructures around the world.

The E-ISAC analysis (2016) identified five themes for defenders to focus on as they consider what this attack means for their organizations in terms of developing an effective resiliency framework that should be construed as opportunities for improvement in resilience: (1) Consider the sequence of events taken by the adversary in the months leading up to the attack without awareness on the part of the victims; (2) Consider the coordinated nature of the attack affecting three target entities and the important opportunities for defenders to disrupt the adversary's sequence of events; (3) Consider the excessive focus on the specific malware used in the attack which placed defenders into a mindset in which they are simply waiting for guidance on attack components so they can eliminate them, rather than recognizing that attacks can be enabled by a variety of approaches; (4) Consider that many capabilities that were demonstrated throughout this attack, and they all provide specific lessons learned for defenders to take action on; (5) Consider information sharing as a key in the identification of a coordinated attack such as ISACs (Information Sharing and Analysis Centers), to enhance situation awareness, which will in turn lead to earlier attack detection and facilitate incident response. The operator at Prykarpattyaoblenergo could not have known what that little flicker of his mouse cursor portended that day. But now the people in charge of the world's power supplies have been warned. This attack was relatively short-lived and benign. The next one might not be (Zetter, 2016a).

This case illustrates that a cyber resilience framework as described in this book would have assisted in mitigating or preventing this attack in its entirety by: (1) Organizing a strategy, policy and process for detecting in advance the looming activities of their adversaries; (2) Developing an awareness through cyber training that attacks can be enabled in a variety of ways; and (3) Connecting rapidly with other stakeholders and supply chain actors who might have prevented the short-sightedness and provided immediate guidance or support instead of waiting for guidance on attack components.

9.2. Solar Winds

The most recent devastating cyber attach in 2020 is still under investigation. The SolarWinds breach — in which suspected Russia-backed hackers concealed malware in software updates by SolarWinds, a company that serves U.S. government, the UK and private sector entities — has reportedly compromised targets in the National Institutes of Health and the Departments of Commerce, Treasury, Defense, State and Homeland Security. Though the breach is still being investigated, the early signs indicate the reach of the stealthy supply-chain attack will have substantial aftershocks. SolarWinds claims to have 300,000 customers, including the National Security Agency, all five branches of the U.S. military, and entities in the health, technology, telecommunications, media, and finance sectors. Clearly, this is a case where cyber resilience failed and until there is a full investigation and legal proceedings against the attackers a complete analysis of the reasons for the failure will remain uncertain. This attack which may be one of the worst in history creates increasing focus on the importance of cyber resilience. Just as frightening as the scope of the attack is how smoothly the attack circumvented government and private-sector cyber defenses (Morris and Hackett, 2021). Some see the attack not as a failure by one software vendor, but as an indictment of U.S. cybersecurity itself. Whatever its consequences turn out to be, the SolarWinds hack has exposed major flaws in the patchwork public-private partnership we've relied on to keep our information technology safe, drawing attention to just how ill-coordinated and permeable it can be.

In the traditional defense supply chain— the makers of fighter jets or Coast Guard cutters—private contractors submit to strict oversight and rigorous standards in exchange for long-term, high-value government contracts. In cybersecurity, in contrast, a handful of midsize government agencies work with a vastly larger constellation of private software developers, cybersecurity contractors, and their customers, offering relatively few guidelines and imposing only loose oversight (Morris and Hackett, 2021). Most experts in the industry view the decentralized, market-driven structure of U.S. cybersecurity as a source of agility and innovation. But in the SolarWinds debacle, they also see the system's weaknesses on full display. In this mega-breach, the industry's flawed financial incentives, a lack of transparency, underinvestment in training, and old-fashioned cost-cutting each played a role. These failures encapsulate the challenge of fixing America's cybersecurity structure. The encouraging news is that corporate and public-sector reformers are already responding with repairs and countermeasures; the less good news is that many of those repair efforts are in their earliest days (Morris and Hackett, 2021).

Clearly lacking here as noted by expert evaluation thus far was a cyber resilience framework that would have provided a more complete understanding of the supply chain visibility including the fact that their own cyber security vendors were incapable of detecting or mitigating the attacks before serious and extensive damage was done described by a leading technology firm as the worst cyber-attack in history (Microsoft Blog, 2020). Moreover, better data and shared tracking tools among stakeholders would have expedited the response time and prevented not only the serious delay in discovery of the magnitude of the incident but also a better coordination among the multiple users of Solar Wind's software. This case raises the important question of secondary risk. How do we better ensure that our supply chain is resilient without regular reviews of data and evaluation and optimization of our supply chain.

9.3. The Office of Personal Management Data Breach and U.S. Intelligence

Though Solar Winds may be the most serious cyber-attack in history, the Office of Personnel Management Data Breach has been described as the worst in the history of cyber-attacks against the U.S. government. In May 2015, the federal Office of Personnel Management (OPM) reported a breach affecting 4.2 million current and former federal employees reported widely as the most potentially damaging cyber heists in U.S. government history because of the abundant detail in the files (Fruhlinger, 2020). A few days later, it revealed a second breach. The second breach brought the number impacted to 22 million people who had applied for government jobs or security clearances (H.R., 2016). More than five million digital fingerprints were compromised, giving rise to concern about the security of biometrics. Members of law enforcement, the intelligence community and the federal court system were all impacted. Some of the data included information on finances, peoples' sex lives, drug and alcohol problems and debts, all of which could be used for blackmail (H.R., 2016).

The U.S. House of Representatives Committee on Oversight and Government Reform issued a Report on September 7, 2016, after an extensive investigation of the OPM Data Breach (HR, 2016). The Report concluded that the agency failed to prioritize cybersecurity and adequately secure high value data, "*despite years of warnings from the Inspector General*" (ix). The conduct of the Agency "*represents a failure of culture and leadership, not technology*" (ix). Moreover, "*the exfiltration of the security clearance files could have been prevented*" (vii).

The Report included 13 recommendations. Many of which are relevant not just to OPM Agency's cybersecurity but to the cyber resilience of the OPM at the time of the attack and following the attack (H.R. 2016, pp. 20-27). Among the recommendations are the following:

- Each federal agency must ensure agency CIOs are empowered, accountable, competent, and retained for more than the current average two-year tenure (p. 20).

- OMB should provide guidance to agencies to promote a zero trust IT security model (p. 20).
- The federal agencies should reduce the use of social security numbers (SSN) in order to mitigate the risk of identity theft (p. 21).
- Clear rules for accountability and dedicated funding should be established by the end of FY 2017 to ensure the U.S. Department of Defense (DoD) is successful in securing the background investigation materials (p. 22).
- Congress should encourage federal agencies to provide federal employees with financial education and counseling services that are designed to help employees recognize, prevent, and mitigate identify theft through existing Employee Assistance Programs (EAP).
- Recruiting, training, and retaining cyber security specialists should be a critical national security priority (p. 26).

The impact of the OPM attack has been widespread and demonstrates that a resilience framework that does not address the privacy and human rights of its users can cause serious personal damage to people's lives and may have endangered permanently the lives of millions of government employees through identity theft, property extortion, and numerous other serious crimes. OPM was also not able to attribute the activity quickly through better interaction with all its stakeholders before the second breach occurred. This attack like so many others raises the question of espionage related attacks where national security trumps protection of privacy requiring different frameworks including strategies and approaches that will provide more transparency of the dangers to the users as well as greater respect for the human impact of these attacks.

9.4. 4. Sony Pictures: An International Wrongful Act

On November 24, 2014, a group calling itself The Guardians of Peace (GOP) managed to breach Sony Pictures Entertainment and bring their systems down to a screeching halt after release of the film, "The Interview.". Resulting from this breach the GOP claims to have stolen over 100 terabytes of data containing Social Security numbers, salaries, movies, and other personally identifiable information. Within days, the stolen data was posted on the Internet along with demands from the GOP group that included not releasing The Interview.

The Sony 2014 cyber-attack highlights the need for a cyber resilience framework that incorporates strategic, operational, and tactical level engagement in countering cyberattacks. This case highlights the multiple things that can go wrong simultaneously within a short time frame that could have been easily addressed through better support from Sony sponsorship and a strategy and governance process for not only cyber-attack prevention but mitigation once the attack is in process (Sanchez, 2015). Despite the efforts of organizations such as NATO, the OECD, the UN, and the G8 and the G20 cyber working groups and alliances, no treaty exists to regulate cyber-attacks. Though there is consensus across the G8 that "unauthorized access" should be illegal, it is not clear what constitutes "unauthorized access" and the right to respond.

This was not the first serious attack against Sony as earlier cyber-attacks had occurred in 2011 which unfortunately did not sufficiently change the lax culture at

Sony about cyber security. According to Stuart Thomas, who previously built the PlayStation 2 network for Sony in 2001, the biggest mistake Sony made that led to the Play Station Network hacks was its organizational complexity and a lack of proper security support at the board level (VentureBeat, 2011).

The impact of the 2014 attack on people's lives was heightened by the lack of transparency and communication on the part of Sony. As expressed at the time, since Sony suffered its hack attack, the company has issued very little information with respect to the breach, except to say that it was "*a very sophisticated cyberattack*" (Schwartz, 2014). A detailed analysis by Sans Institute revealed that with Sony Pictures insufficient malware defenses, monitoring, audit logs, encryption, controlled use of administrative credentials, and incident response contributed to the massive breach of the organization (Sanchez, 2015). Moreover, the breach against Sony Pictures Entertainment in 2014 by the GOP brought the entire organization down and led to the leaking of sensitive data on the Internet. Not only was sensitive data leaked but the GOP inserted wiper malware into the infrastructure that essentially made bricks out of Sony's computer systems. Sony Pictures Entertainment was forced to scramble to bring the infrastructure back up while dealing with the massive number of sensitive documents affecting employees and the organization. In addition, Sony's response about suing media outlets for publishing information did not help with their stance of wanting to improve security. This dilemma between protecting critical infrastructure while at the same time protecting privacy rights of millions of employees within the organization is a common one and priorities clearly need to be understood by all stakeholders in the event one must give way for the other.

Using our model framework, Table 9.2 illustrates the need for a resilience framework based on the findings from the U.S. Congress Oversight Committee and private company investigations that show that each of the attacks could have been mitigated or in most cases prevented if a cyber resilience framework had been implemented.

The Sony Pictures cyber-attack deemed to be the most damaging and the biggest cyber-attack at the time in the United States, raised the question of cyber-attacks that may constitute an act of war. In 2014, NATO members formally affirmed cyber defense as part of member states' "collective defense obligations" under Article 5 of the NATO Charter at the 2014 Wales Summit. However, they did not define exactly when an attack would trigger such obligations, saying in a joint statement, "*[a] decision as to when a cyber-attack would lead to the invocation of Article 5 would be taken by the North Atlantic Council on a case-by-case basis*" (Daugirdas & Moretenson, 2015). Even if the Sony hack did not constitute an armed attack, Tallinn Manual principles suggest that confirmed North Korean involvement would still constitute a violation of U.S. sovereignty and therefore an "internationally wrongful act" (NATO, CCDCOE, 2017). If so, the United States would be entitled under the International Law Commission (2021) Articles on State Responsibility to take countermeasures "*commensurate with the injury suffered, taking into account the gravity of the internationally wrongful act and the rights in question*" (ILC, 2021). In this regard, the escalation of sanctions against individuals and entities connected with the North Korean government has been the primary public U.S. response to the attack (US Department of Treasury, 2019).

Table 9.2: *Application of the Resilience Framework to Catastrophic Breaches*

Event	2014 U.S. OPM Data Breach	2014 Sony Attacks	2015 The Ukrainian Power Grid	2020 Solar Wind Hack
Organize	Documents and testimony proving OPM IS posture was undermined by a woefully unsecure IT environment, internal politics and bureaucracy, and misplaced priorities related to the deployment of security tools that slowed vital security decisions. (HR, 2016, p. viii).	This was not the first serious attack against Sony as earlier cyber-attacks had occurred in 2011 which unfortunately did not sufficiently change the lax culture at Sony about cyber security (Sanchez, 2015).	The excessive focus on the specific malware used in the attack placed the defenders into a mindset in which they are simply waiting for guidance on attack components so they can eliminate them, rather than recognizing that attacks can be enabled by a variety of approaches (E-ISAC, 2016).	Some see the attack not as a failure of a software vendor, but as an indictment of U.S. cybersecurity itself (Morris and Hackett, 2021)
Develop	The longstanding failure of OPMs leadership to implement basic cyber hygiene represents a failure of culture and leadership (HR, 2016, p. ix)	A detailed analysis by Sans Institute revealed that with Sony Pictures insufficient malware defenses, monitoring, audit logs, encryption, controlled use of administrative credentials, and incident response contributed to the massive breach on the organization (Sanchez, 2015).	The analysis of the Ukraine attack revealed many opportunities to stop or prevent this attack (Zetter, 2016a).	In this mega-breach, the industry's flawed financial incentives, a lack of transparency, under investment in training and old-fashioned cost-cutting each played a role.
Regulate	Reprioritize federal information security efforts towards a zero trust model. (HR, 2016, p. 20).	Not being a financial services or health care company Sony wasnt required to meet specific and detailed regulatory requirements for data security involving personal data presenting a gap in oversight policy (Wiley, 2015).	The lack of an international treaty or regulatory mechanism presented an opportunity for hostile actors to intrude without fear of retribution of retaliation.	Though rigorous standards exist in highly critical industries such as defense, in cyber security a handful of midsize government agencies work with a vastly larger constellation of private software developers, cybersecurity contractors and their customers offering loose oversight (Morris and Hackett, 2021)
Connect	The Data Breach should have sounded a high-level multi-agency national security alarm (HR, 2016, p. viii)	Since Sony suffered its hack attack, the company has issued very little information with respect to the breach, except to say that it was a very sophisticated cyberattack (Schwartz, 2014).	Information sharing was a key in the identification of a coordinated attack to enhance situation awareness, which will in turn lead to earlier attack detection and facilitate incident response (Zetter, 2016a).	The interconnectivity of the cyber security provider to large numbers of organizations from both the public and private sectors exposes " major flaws in the patchwork public-private partnership" Katie Moussouris quoted in (Morris and Hackett, 2021)

9.5.   The Role of Cyber Resilience in Preventing Catastrophic Loss

As reflected in the case summaries discussed in this chapter each of these cyber-attacks was preventable. They all involved serious catastrophic loss, however, not all are capable of attribution at this time.   If we look at the common elements of resilience to adapt, withstand, reduce magnitude and duration of attack, and restore to a new normalization, from the evidence elicited so far it does not appear that resilience was effective in accomplishing these goals. The fact that in all these cyber-attacks the duration was sufficient to cause serious damage and in the case of the 2020 Solar Wind Hack it is not clear that the attack has ended, and the concern of ongoing serious damage persists (Microsoft Blog, 2020). Moreover, there has been no formal attribution to date thus expanding the time frame for additional harm. At the strategic level, resilience requires clear roles, responsibilities, and accountability. Until there is accountability resilience has not achieved its goals. In the four cyber-attacks described in Table 9.1, only one has resulted in economic sanctions. Without a formal trial, the indictments will have little meaning in terms of deferring future behavior particularly if the countries backing the hackers refuse to hold the perpetrators accountable. Without accountability and serious penalties, the cyber-attackers can remain active with the support of their national governments. Particularly, if the countries impacted do not bring actions against the involved nation states. This calls out for a remedy in the form of an international tribunal to bring these criminals to trial.

9.6.   Summary: High Reliability Theory and Mindful Organizing

We conclude this chapter on catastrophic loss by looking at what organizations that avoid failure in high-risk activities do to maintain reliability. A high-reliability organization (HRO) is an organization that has succeeded in avoiding catastrophes despite a high level of risk and complexity. Specific examples that have been studied, most famously by researchers Karl Weick and Kathleen Sutcliffe, include nuclear power plants, air traffic control systems, and naval aircraft carriers. Recently healthcare organizations have moved to adopt the HRO mindset as well. In each case, even a minor error could have catastrophic consequences. According to Weick & Sutcliffe, (2015) so-called high-reliability organizations (HROs) demonstrate particular characteristics in the way they operate: anticipating problems (being aware of what is happening in the work system; being alert to ways in which an incident could occur; looking beyond simplistic explanations for incidents); and containing problems (being prepared to deal with contingencies; using relevant expertise regardless of where it is situated within the organizational hierarchy). In their research on "high reliability organizations" they analyzed how highly regulated and standardized organizations such as nuclear plants, aircraft carriers and firefighting units achieve resilience in a complex environment. They found that technical checklists were not the key to success but instead a list of cultural features they define as "mindful organizing." They identified five principles that include preoccupation with failure, a reluctance to simplify, a sensitivity to operations, a commitment to resilience and a deference to expertise as a shared set of values that foster resilience through constant communication and recalibration in the face of unknowable risks (Weick & Sutcliffe, 2015).

Vogus & Sutcliffe (2012) proposed "mindful organizing" as a collective mental orientation in which the organization continually engages with its environment, re-organizing its structures and activities as necessary, rather than mindlessly executing plans in ignorance of the prevailing circumstances. This is a dynamic social process, consisting of specific actions and interactions between those engaged in frontline organizational work. It creates the context for thought and behavior across the organization but is relatively transient and so needs to be actively maintained. Hopkins (2014) argues that the characteristics of a HRO and the components of safety culture (reporting; flexibility; learning; fairness) are broadly equivalent from the perspective of the field of safety science. High reliability theory should be explored in the cyber field because of the high potential for catastrophic outcomes from a cyber incidence. For instance, a cyber-attack on a nuclear plant could have long lasting and deadly consequences. As reflected in the cases explored in this chapter catastrophic losses from a cyber-attack are real and continue to threaten our businesses, public organizations, and many critical industries where cyber resilience is essential to adaptation and often long recovery periods.

Chapter 10

Case Study Frameworks for Cyber Resilience: Resilience in the Financial Services Sector

Digital freedom stops where that of users begins... Nowadays, digital evolution must no longer be offered to a customer in trade-off between privacy and security. Privacy is not for sale, it's a valuable asset to protect.

Stéphane Nappo - Global Head Information Security Société Générale

In the next 2 chapters effective approaches and solutions for cyber resilience are discussed as well as cyber resilience strategies, policies and technologies that support broader cyber resilience objectives by reviewing case studies in the Banking and Health Care Industries. We begin with a focus in this chapter of the Banking and Financial Services Sector as it has become a major target for cyber criminals and has serious economic and financial impacts. Cyber-attacks are an increasing concern especially for financial service firms which may experience up to 300 times more cyber-attacks per year than other firms (BCG, 2019). Cyber events threaten financial stability through their direct costs as well as through the spillovers they cause. While cyber events show similarity to other types of shocks, cyber events are different along specific dimensions (Healey, et al., 2018). The asymmetric information resulting from a cyber event also creates the potential for beneficial policy intervention. Ex ante, requirements to disclose to regulators even minor cyber events or to share with other banks information on threat assessments and contingency plans could increase resilience by reducing uncertainty and improving collective learning.

10.1. Global Regulation of Resilience in the Financial Services Industry

There is broad agreement that the financial sector should embrace operational resilience in order to withstand and recover from nonfinancial shocks and to protect financial stability. In February 2020, Christine Lagarde, the former managing director of the IMF and now head of the ECB, warned that a cyber-attack had the potential to trigger a liquidity crisis (Winder, 2020). Just how operational resilience should be implemented and achieved remains unclear and is subject to different opinions. The main problem in the financial services industry is not the lack of resources or the ability to implement technical solutions, but the collective action problem: how best to organize the system's protection across governments, financial authorities, and industry and how best to leverage these resources, effectively and efficiently (Maurer and Nelson, 2020).

The Bank for International Settlements (BIS) and the International Organization for Securities Commissions (OICU-IOSCO, 2020) issued guidelines in 2016 on cyber resilience to address the safe and efficient operation of financial market infrastructures (FMIs) in light of numerous attacks on the industry in recent years (BIS, 2016). The guidelines introduced five primary risk management categories and three overarching components that should be addressed across a FMIs cyber resilience framework. The risk management categories are governance; identification; protection; detection; and response and recovery. The overarching components are testing; situational awareness; and learning and evolving. In order to achieve resilience objectives, investments across these guidance categories can be mutually reinforcing and should be considered jointly (BIS, 2016).

Though the categories overlap in part with the National Institute of Standards and Technology (NIST) Standards, recognized worldwide as a benchmark for best cyber practices, there are important differences in these standards. Four years after issuing the Guidelines in August 2020, the Basel Committee on Banking Supervision issued for comment Principles for Operational Resilience. Even prior to the Covid-19 pandemic, the Basel Committee considered that significant operational disruptions would inevitably test improvements to the financial system's resilience made since the Global Financial Crisis (GFC) of 2007-2009. As the Covid-19 pandemic progressed, the Committee observed banks rapidly adapting their operational posture in response to new hazards or changes in existing hazards that occurred in different parts of their organization. Recognizing that a range of potential hazards cannot be prevented, the Committee believed that a pragmatic, flexible approach to operational resilience can enhance the ability of banks to withstand, adapt to, and recover from potential hazards and thereby mitigate potentially severe adverse impacts (BIS, 2020).

National standards for banking regulation for cyber resilience vary widely. Singapore has taken a particularly aggressive approach on resilience. The Monetary Authority of Singapore (MAS) has issued guidance and advisories to address operational, technology and cyber risks. MAS has also focused on surveillance, supervision, and enforcement efforts on financial institutions' pandemic response as well as operational and cyber resilience. The Authority has been aggressive in monitoring the impact of COVID-19, by putting in place additional measures and advisories because of the high level of risk for cyber intrusion (Singapore, 2020).

10.2. Bank of England Setting Tolerance Standards for Resilience

The Bank of England in 2019 set new standards for operational resilience of its Banks in the event of a severe cyber-attack. In the March 2019 Record of the Bank's Financial Policy Committee (FPC), the Bank restated its agreement from June 2018 'that as part of establishing clear baseline expectations, it would set tolerances for how quickly critical financial companies must be able to restore vital financial services following a severe but plausible cyber incident.' Consistent with the FPC's remit, these would be calibrated to ensure financial stability and avoid material economic harm. As such, 'the tolerances would not imply zero tolerance for disruption'. For situations where we want to assess, at a high level, a firm's cyber resilience capability, the PRA and FCA have created a questionnaire.

CQUEST consists of multiple-choice questions covering all aspects of cyber resilience, such as:

- Does the firm have a board-approved cyber security strategy?
- How does it identify and protect its critical assets?
- How does it detect and respond to an incident, recover the business, and learn from the experience?

While significantly higher levels of capital and liquidity have improved banks' ability to absorb financial shocks, the Committee believes that further work is necessary to strengthen banks' ability to absorb operational risk-related events, such as pandemics, cyber incidents, technology failures or natural disasters, which could cause significant operational failures or wide-scale disruptions in financial markets (BoE, 2019).

10.3. The European Central Banks

In March 2017, the Governing Council of the ECB approved the "Euro system cyber resilience strategy for FMIs". The objective of this strategy is to improve the cyber resilience of the euro area financial sector as a whole by enhancing the "cyber readiness" of individual FMIs that are overseen by the Euro system central banks, and to foster collaboration among FMIs, their critical service suppliers and the authorities. Specifically, the strategy aims to put the Guidance into practice and comprises three pillars. The evolving nature of cyberattacks makes it necessary to ensure that FMIs strengthen their individual level of cyber maturity. In this regard, Pillar 1 (FMI Readiness) aims to ensure that the Guidance is put into practice in a consistent manner, by implementing a harmonized approach to assessing FMIs in the euro area against the Guidance. To facilitate this process, the ECB has—among other things —developed the Cyber Resilience Oversight Expectations (CROE). The CROE serves three key purposes: (i) it provides FMIs with detailed steps on how to operationalize the Guidance, ensuring they are able to foster improvements and enhance their cyber resilience over a sustained period of time; (ii) it provides overseers with clear expectations to assess FMIs under their responsibility; and (iii) it provides the basis for a meaningful discussion between the FMIs and their respective overseers (ECB, 2018).

10.4. Financial Cyber Resilience Regulation in the United States

The Federal Reserve Bank defines "operational resilience" in the financial sector as the ability to deliver operations, including critical operations and core business lines, through a disruption from any hazard. It is the outcome of effective operational risk management combined with sufficient financial and operational resources to prepare, adapt, withstand, and recover from disruptions (FRB, 2020). The Bank rightly recognizes that while potential hazards may not be prevented, a flexible operational resilience approach can enhance the ability of firms to recover from an attack and continue operations. A top priority of the Federal Reserve is the recognition of the global and interconnected nature of banks and the importance of supervisory coordination, and that the Bank has demonstrated its commitment to working closely with the European Central Bank and the UK Prudential

Regulatory Authority through various initiatives to ensure that supervisory approaches on operational resilience are well coordinated.

10.5. Financial Regulation in Developing Countries

The Financial Inclusion Global Initiative (FIGI) was launched by the World Bank Group, the International Telecommunication Union (ITU) and the Committee on Payments and Market Infrastructures (CPMI), to advance financial inclusion in developing countries. The FIGI initiative comprises 3 working groups (WG), the Digital Identity WG, Electronic Payments Acceptance WG, and Security, Infrastructure and Trust WG. Under the Security, Infrastructure and Trust Working Group, there is a dedicated workstream focus on cyber security for Financial Market Infrastructures (FMIs), to improve the cyber resilience of systems critical to financial stability and financial inclusion, especially in developing countries (World Bank, 2019).

10.6. The Financial Sector: Case Studies in Cyber Resilience

For cybercriminals, companies in the financial sector are attractive targets because hackers can obtain money directly without having to deal with the complexities of selling stolen goods. It is little surprise that this industry, at least according to research from Dimension Data, suffers more attacks than any other sector. A major attack on the industry occurred in 2014, when hackers targeted JP Morgan, stealing data relating to more than 76 million private customers, and seven million businesses. Meanwhile, in February 2016, criminals stole 81 million US Dollars in an audacious robbery when they successfully hacked the SWIFT system of the central bank in Bangladesh. A similar heist occurred two years later when the Indian City Union Bank noticed that its systems had been hacked and 1.5 million Euros had been transferred to international banks without authorization. Table 10.1 summarizes the framework for each of these cases.

Table 10.1: *Application of the Cyber Resilience Framework to the Financial Sector*

Event	Organize	Develop	Regulate	Connect
2015 Bangladesh Bank Hack	The success of the hackers was, more than anything else, down to weaknesses in the institutions they robbed (Aon, 2020).	The delay in communication caused the hackers to exploit the system without interruption.	The heist revealed that the New York Fed lacked a system for spotting potential fraud in real time – even though such systems are used elsewhere – instead, relying at times on checking payments after they were made, usually for problems such as violating U.S. sanctions (Das and Spicer, 2016).	The relationship between the SWIFT network, the Bangladesh Bank, and the Federal Reserve in New York indicated weaknesses among all 3 systems in terms of cyber security and a lack of awareness and notification of the takeover attack (Finkle & Quadir, 2016)

Event	Organize	Develop	Regulate	Connect
2016 Tesco Bank	The UK Financial Conduct Authority found that Tesco Bank could have ended the attack much earlier than it did (UK FCA, 2018).	The FCA key findings concluded that Tesco Bank did not respond to the cyber-attack with sufficient "rigor, skill and urgency" (UK FCA, 2018).	The £16.4 million fine imposed by the UK FCA on Tesco Personnel provides a salutary lesson on the regulatory exposure associated with failing adequately to prepare for and respond to a cyber-attack (UK FCA, 2018).	No communication between the Bank's Financial Crime Operations Team and the Bank Fraud Team for a full 24 hours after the attack began caused escalation in the damage (UK FCA, 2018).
2017 Equifax	Equifax failed to implement clear lines of authority (HR, 2018) causing a lack of accountability and failure of management structure	A failure to implement responsible security measurements showed a lack of leadership and training (Senate, 2019)	The vulnerability was known two months before and the U.S. Senate Report cited the company as an example of how negligence and ignorance undermine any approach to resilience. (Senate, 2019)	The attack impacted the security of 147M U.S. Citizens, and the findings determined that Equifax was unprepared to support affected consumers. Equifax waited six weeks to inform the public (Senate, 2019)

10.6.1. Equifax Attack: America's Largest Credit Bureau

The 2017 Equifax Data Breach of the American credit reporting agency was one of the biggest of its kind in history affecting 148 million consumers including some in Europe. In February 2020, the U.S. charged 4 members of the Chinese military with responsibility for the attack (DOJ, 2020c). The indictment also charged the defendants with stealing trade secret information, namely Equifax's data compilations and database designs. As described by Attorney General Barr, "*in short, this was an organized and remarkably brazen criminal heist of sensitive information of nearly half of all Americans, as well as the hard work and intellectual property of an American company, by a unit of the Chinese military.*"

According to the U.S. House of Representatives Committee on Oversight and Government Reform on May 13, 2017, attackers began a cyberattack on Equifax that lasted for 76 days (HR, 2018). On September 7, 2017, Equifax announced a cybersecurity incident affecting 143 million consumers. This number eventually grew to 148 million—nearly half the U.S. population and 56 percent of American adults.

The breached information included social security numbers, names, dates of birth, addresses, credit card numbers, and in some cases, driver's license numbers. For this attack, hackers took advantage of a security vulnerability in the open-source framework Apache Struts, which formed part of Equifax's IT infrastructure. This was a known vulnerability, which had been discovered two months previously. Unfortunately, Equifax had not installed the patch that had been issued to close this vulnerability (Senate, 2019).

A 2019 U.S. Senate Report identified several gaps in Equifax's security architecture, singling out the company as an example of how negligence and ignorance diminish a company's cyber security posture, not to mention undermine any approach to resilience (if such an approach even existed). Moreover, Equifax's shortcomings are long-standing and reflect a broader culture of complacency toward cybersecurity preparedness. The Subcommittee also lacks a full understanding of the breach, as the company failed to preserve relevant messages sent over an internal messaging platform (Senate, 2019). Important recommendations from the Senate investigation were that Congress should pass legislation that establishes a national uniform standard requiring private entities that collect and store PII to take reasonable and appropriate steps to prevent cyberattacks and data breaches, and that private entities that suffer a data breach should be required to notify affected consumers, law enforcement, and the appropriate federal regulatory agency without unreasonable delay (Senate, 2019). In the United States there is no national uniform standard requiring a private entity to notify affected individuals in the event of a data breach. All 50 states, the District of Columbia, Guam, Puerto Rico, and the Virgin Islands have enacted legislation requiring data breach notification laws. In the absence of a national standard, states have taken significantly different approaches to notification standards with different triggers for notifications and different timelines for notifying individuals whose information has been stolen or improperly disclosed.

In 2018 the U.S. House Oversight Committee released a staff report on the causes of the breach that concluded that the Equifax breach was "entirely preventable." The report includes many notable findings, including recommendations for the business sector to avoid such incidents in the future. The findings determined that Equifax failed to define clear lines of authority assigning responsibility for the data it was collecting leading to an execution gap between IT policy development and operation, that it was using complex and outdated systems, that it failed to implement responsible security measurements including allowing over 300 security certificates to expire, and that it was unprepared to support affected customers in the event of a breach (HR, 2018).

The Accountability of Equifax for its failures remains controversial as the damage continues to have impact to consumers in the U.S. and Europe. In the weeks following the breach, Equifax let go of not one, but three of its top executives. Several other employees were charged with insider trading in relation to the breach. Equifax's image, as a result of the scandal, took a serious beating that was more than reflected in the stock market, however, there are many that feel that was insufficient. In addition, the State Attorneys General in the United States secured a settlement with Equifax that includes a Consumer Restitution Fund of up to $425 million, a $175 million payment to the states, and injunctive relief, which also includes a significant financial commitment (Oregon, 2019).

The Committee found that Equifax has "a heightened responsibility" to protect the personal data of its customers, it also emphasized that the government should be more involved as well. It recommended organizations increase oversight, accountability, and transparency in their operations and infrastructure, and modernize IT security solutions. From the European side because it occurred in the pre-GDPR era, European authorities – on behalf of affected UK customers – could only fine the company the maximum allowable penalty under the 1996 Data Protection Act: £500,000. Under the GDPR, that penalty would have been orders of magnitude higher.

10.6.2. *Canada's Investigation into the Equifax Breach*

Canada's investigation into the Equifax Breach found safeguards were lacking in the following four areas: (1) vulnerability management; (2) network segregation; (3) implementation of basic information security practices; and (4) oversight (Canada, 2019). Since the process of resilience is intricately linked to cyber security practices these four violations of security practice made the ability to identify the attacker, respond to the attack and curtail the attacker that much more difficult not to mention the complexity of the recovery itself. With respect to identifying rules, regulations and standards that must be complied with, Equifax Canada indicated that its legal and privacy team had provided training for Equifax Inc. staff on Canadian legal and regulatory requirements including privacy (Canada, 2019). In addition, Equifax Inc. conducts an annual review of its data security policies, which the Equifax Canada CPO contributes to from the perspective of Canadian requirements. However, it was unable to describe any of these contributions, citing that all documentation of any such contributions had been purged due to its one-year retention policy for internal emails. This case study highlights major problems in cyber resilience that include a failure to implement procedures despite training, a total disregard for accountability mechanisms, and a failure to enforce regulatory requirements. All human error that could have prevented the attack.

10.6.3. *Tesco Bank*

There are several important examples on the failure of resiliency gleaned from the cyber-attack on Tesco Bank in November 2016. As highlighted in the UK Financial Conduct Authority's final notice to Tesco assessing a financial penalty of £16.4 million Tesco had failed to follow procedures and *"respond to the cyber-attack with sufficient rigour, skill and urgency"* (UK FCA, 2018, p. 20). As described in the notice Tesco Bank inadvertently issued debit cards with sequential PAN numbers. This increased the likelihood that the attackers would find the next PAN number in the sequence. It took 21 hours after the attack began before Tesco Bank's Fraud Strategy Team was informed about the incident. Only after what the FCA describes as a "series of errors" -- including Tesco Bank's Financial Crime Operations Team sending an email to the wrong address, instead of making a phone call as procedure requires -- was the fraud team made aware of the attack (UK FCA, 2018, pp. 1-2). In all that time, nothing had been done to stop the attacks, with fraudulent transactions continuing to siphon money from accounts as the bank received more and more calls from worried customers.

It was only once the Fraud Strategy Team had finally been alerted that some headway was made into countering the attack. It was found that the vast majority of transactions were coming from Brazil and were using a payment method known as 'PoS 91' -- making transactions based on magnetic stripes that carry identifying information about the debit card. Once PoS 91 was identified as the most frequently used channel for fraudulent transactions and Brazil as the location they were occurring, Tesco Bank's Fraud Strategy Team put a rule in place to block those transactions from 1:48am on Sunday 6th November -- almost a full 24 hours after the attack began (UK FCA, 2018, p. 2).

This case highlights the problem of the normalization of deviance, the failure to follow established procedures over a period of time such that the behavior becomes normalized (Vaughan, 2016). The decision to send an email rather than call as established by the procedures was an example of how laxness in following process can lead to a disaster in this case a cyber breach. The breach revealed serious weaknesses in the operation of Tesco Bank's financial crime controls. The failure to take steps to address these weaknesses left Tesco Bank's personal current account customers vulnerable to fraudulent PoS 91 transactions. Tesco Bank was aware that its debit card systems were vulnerable to PoS 91 transactions but failed to implement specific authentication and fraud detection rules to prevent such transactions. Tesco Bank is in the business of banking and fundamental to that business is protecting its customers from financial crime (UK FCA, 2018, p.23).

Moreover, this case highlights the need for a cyber resilience framework that requires the development of an organizational structure, leadership team, regulation and oversight, and connections with both internal and external stakeholders including its own fraud team so that prompt solutions can be found preventing the serious escalation in damage that occurred here (p. 23).

10.6.4. Bangladesh Bank Hack in Dahka

The February 2015 cyber-attack on Bangladesh's central bank that let hackers steal over $80 million from the institutes' Federal Reserve bank account was reportedly caused by the malware installed on the Bank's computer systems. The attack is considered one of the largest bank heists of all time. SWIFT, a cooperative owned by 3,000 financial institutions, confirmed to major news agencies that it was aware of malware targeting its client software. However, the delay in communication caused the hackers to exploit the system without interruption. The evidence suggests that hackers manipulated the Alliance Access server software, which banks use to interface with SWIFT's messaging platform, in a bid to cover up fraudulent transfers that had been previously ordered (Finkle & Quadir, 2016). The findings from BAE and SWIFT do not explain how the fraudulent orders were created and pushed through the system. That remains a key mystery in ongoing probes into the heist. Also, undetermined is the identity of the hackers and the investigation has not identified any connection with the acts of a nation state. The attack caused serious economic harm, but no loss of life. Thus, the international community has not classified the attack as an armed attack triggering the right to self-defense under Article 51 of the United Nations Charter.

The thieves were organized, well networked, and well-funded. But their success was, more than anything else, due to weaknesses in the institutions they robbed (Aon, 2020). The theft involved manipulating the SWIFT system – a digital messaging platform that manages many of the world's interbank financial transfers – to fool the New York branch of the U.S. Federal Reserve (which holds many international banking assets) into transferring funds to accounts owned by the thieves. Pretending to be the BCB, the thieves sent fake instructions over SWIFT to the

New York Fed, asking for some funds to be transferred to bank accounts in Southeast Asia. Banks should be using the very same controls over their own systems that they expect of their own customers (Kitten and Schwartz, 2016).

As described by Kim Zetter, (2016b) an American investigative reporter and journalist, on the morning of Friday, February 5, the director of the bank found the printer tray empty. When bank workers tried to print the reports manually, they couldn't. The software on the terminal that connects to the SWIFT network indicated that a critical system file was missing or had been altered. When they finally got the software working the next day and were able to restart the printer, dozens of suspicious transactions spit out. The Fed bank in New York had apparently sent queries to Bangladesh Bank questioning dozens of the transfer orders, but no one in Bangladesh had responded. The attackers timed that attack well since the Fed Reserve Bank was closed for the weekend. Banks should conduct SWIFT transactions only on computers that are isolated from other devices on their networks, says Sean Sullivan, an adviser at the security firm F-Secure. This case illustrates the criticality of cyber resilience where there are serious time lapses, an absence of response due to weekend closures, and a failure to adapt to and recover in time to prevent serious losses. There were many human errors that brought about the disastrous outcome in this case that could have been easily prevented with a more resilient approach to its banking operations at the strategic, operational, and tactical levels.

10.7. Summary: The Future of Cyber Resilience in the Financial Services Industry

In 2018 the U.S. Department of Justice charged 36 individuals for their alleged roles in the Infraud Organization, an Internet-based cybercriminal enterprise engaged in the large-scale acquisition, sale, and dissemination of stolen identities, compromised debit and credit cards, personally identifiable information, financial and banking information, computer malware, and other contraband (DOJ, 2018). Too often financial crimes go unpunished due to problems of attribution, weaknesses in the financial system's cyber security and resilience practices, and the lack of regulation over cyber conduct in the industry. The culture of financial institutions has not boded well for the implementation of cyber resilient practices.

As discussed in this chapter, the financial services industry must consider dramatic changes to ensure the serious cyber-attacks we have witnessed over the past decade do not occur moving forward. The Carnegie Endowment for International Peace through the World Economic Forum had recently sponsored research on international strategies to better protect the financial system against cyber threats (Maurer and Nelson, 2020). The study outlines thirty-two recommendations and forty-four supporting actions to be implemented ideally in the 2021-2024 timeframe (p. 6). There are six core pillars for the recommendations that focus on cyber resilience and include all of the proposed pillars of the cyber resilience framework proposed in this book. These include: (1) cyber resilience; (2) international norms; (3) collective response to disrupt malicious actors and more effectively deter future attacks; (4) development of a cybersecurity workforce to address challenges including limited pipelines and a lack of diversity; (5) alignment and extension of capacity building efforts across all pillars for those seeking assistance; and (6) safeguarding financial inclusion and the G20s achievements of the past decade in this area (pp. 6-7). The critical aspects of this study show the benefits of collective response in disrupting and deterring attackers more effectively which is central to all cyber resilient strategies. If the recommendations are implemented within the proposed deadline of 2024, it should provide vast improvement in the functioning of cyber resilience in the financial services industry particularly as it relates to the developing world.

Chapter 11

Resilience in the Health Care Sector

"It's alarming" that many firms don't have cybersecurity plans.
Harriet Green – IBM Asia Practice: CEO and Chair

The health care industry has lagged behind other industries in protecting its main stakeholder (i.e., its patients), and now hospitals must invest considerable capital and effort in protecting their systems. However, this is easier said than done because hospitals are extraordinarily technology-saturated, complex organizations with high end point complexity, internal politics, and regulatory pressures (Jalali and Kaiser, 2018).

As compared to the financial industry where the issue of cybersecurity has been a major concern for decades, the health field has just recently begun to confront the problem and devote more resources and investment in cyber security and resilience. The potential harm is also far greater due to the type of sensitive information at risk such as unique biometric data and the impact on patient health and safety.

11.1. The Healthcare Industry

Recent healthcare statistics from the World Health Organization (WHO) show that it's one of the largest *and* fastest-growing industries in the world worth 8.5 trillion in 2018 up from 7.8 trillion in 2017 (WHO, 2019). Health care spending according to Deloittes's 2020 Outlook as a share of gross domestic product (GDP) will likely remain at around 10.2 percent through 2023, equal to 2018's ratio (Allen, 2020). This anticipated steady state reflects both economic improvements and health systems' efforts to contain costs (EIU, 2019). On a per capita basis, spending will likely continue to be unevenly spread, ranging from US $12,262 in the United States to just US$45 in Pakistan in 2023 (Allen, 2020). Efforts to close this gap will be hampered by higher population growth in many developing economies. With the 2019 global population of 7.7 billion expected to reach 8.5 billion by 2030 (UN, 2019) meeting health needs won't be easy. However, Asian countries will likely also contribute around half of the global growth in higher-income households (those earning over US $25,000 a year). Population growth, combined with increased economic power and efforts to expand public health systems, will likely result in higher health spending (EIU, 2019). As of 4 May 2020, a total of 23,564 hospitals and health-care facilities in 184 countries or areas have registered their commitment to handle hygiene as part of the World Health Organization's (WHO) global campaign – Save Lives: Clean Your Hands (WHO, 2019).

11.2. Cyber Attacks in the Healthcare Industry

The dangers of cyber-attacks are particularly alarming in the healthcare industry where a failure of a system can become a life-or-death matter. According to the

European Network and Information Security Agency (ENISA, 2020), healthcare organizations were the favorite target of ransomware attackers during all of the previous years, and this trend also continued in 2020. There has been a 45 percent increase in cyber-attacks targeting healthcare organizations globally according to Checkpoint Software Technology (CST), due to the susceptibility of hospitals to ransomware attacks for fast financial gain. This is more than double the increase in cyber-attacks across all other industries worldwide in the same period of time (CST, 2021). While the attacks involved a variety of methods, ransomware has shown the largest increase and is the biggest threat to healthcare organizations, according to the report. An October 2020 alert from the Cybersecurity & Infrastructure Security Agency (CISA), the Federal Bureau of Investigation (FBI), and the Department of Health and Human Services (HHS), reported that the agencies have credible information about an increased and imminent cybercrime threat to U.S. hospitals and healthcare providers. Throughout October 2020, the malware known as Ryuk was heavily attributed to a large number of infections against U.S.-based healthcare entities, a surge that occurred despite a concerted disruption effort by cybersecurity vendors in September 2020 (Crowdstrike, 2021). The same malware was used against Universal Health Services in September 2020 causing hospital personnel to move to an all-paper system due to the attack which left patients being rerouted to other emergency departments and waiting for appointments and test results (Newman, 2020). The attack was undertaken overnight in an effort to encrypt and lock down as many systems as possible. The Checkpoint Report speculates that these ransomware attacks are bringing the hackers cash windfalls which is making them hungrier for more and the world's healthcare system's preoccupation with the COVID-19 pandemic has made the industry a prime target.

Cyberattacks continue to increase in volume and sophistication and measurably impact the healthcare industry which has had some of the worst cyberattacks in terms of personal data extraction in recent years. In the United States as required by section 13402(e)(4) of the HITECH Act, the Secretary must post a list of breaches of unsecured protected health information affecting 500 or more individuals. Cybercriminals who successfully gain access to medical data use it for conducting fraud or identity theft for lucrative purposes. Also, the personal data often includes information on a patient's medical history, which may be used in targeted spear-phishing attacks. As of January 31, 2021, the US Department of Health and Human Services' HIPAA Breach Reporting website showed a total of 78 million breaches since 2009. The number of individuals affected by health data breaches also has surged in recent years. More large healthcare data breaches were reported in 2020 than in any other year since the HITECH Act called for the U.S. Department of Health and Human Services' Office for Civil Rights to start publishing healthcare data breach figures on its website. In 2020, healthcare data breaches of 500 or more records were reported at a rate of more than 1.76 per day with 642 large data breaches reported by healthcare providers, health plans, healthcare clearing houses and business associates of those entities – 25% more than 2019, which was also a record-breaking year. More than twice the number of data breaches are now being reported than 6 years ago and three times the number of data breaches that occurred in 2010.

Based on these statistics, building the cyber resilience of a hospital is vital and it is a shared responsibility. Users (i.e., clinicians and administration staff) should undergo training and should practice digital hygiene, decision makers should enforce the proper policies and consider cybersecurity in purchasing decisions, and manufacturers should equip their products with the appropriate cybersecurity measures. The information security teams of hospitals should also enact and upkeep the proper tools to safeguard the hospital and patients (Argaw et al., 2020).

The information accessed through health data breaches is of particular interest to criminals because of the breadth and detail of medical records. As these records include private data such as name, date of birth, insurance, and health provider information, as well as health and genetic information, it is not possible to restore privacy or to reverse psychosocial harm when private data are compromised (Argaw, et al., 2020, p. 1).

The United Kingdom's National Health System hospitals, which suffered from the WannaCry ransomware attacks in May 2017, were forced to delay treatment plans and even to reroute incoming ambulances because they lost access to hospital information systems (Millard, 2017). Given today's threat landscape in the healthcare industry, and the number of interconnected devices used in hospitals and healthcare facilities, proactive resilience is essential to address the long-term consequences of these attacks.

11.3. Cost of a Data Breach

A key finding in the Ponemon IBM 2019 Cost of a Data Breach Report was that the average total cost of a data breach in the healthcare industry was $6.45 million, or 65 percent higher than the average total cost of a data breach generally. (Ponemon, 2019). Data Breaches in the healthcare industry are not confined to the U.S. In 2015 the European Union Agency for Network and Information Security (ENISA) conducted an eHealth Survey and interviews of its member countries focusing on the approaches and measures taken to protect critical healthcare systems including the availability, continuity and resilience of the systems and infrastructure. The findings indicated that one of the top priorities in security is the management of incidents and the need for a regulatory framework in many member countries. Other concerns included network security access control to protect the integrity and privacy of patients, and business continuity and disaster recovery. Recommendations included compliance with international standards such as ISO and internal and external security audits (ENISA, 2015). In May 2020, the UK's National Cyber-Security Centre announced a significant increase in cyber-attacks perpetrated by hostile states and cyber-criminals targeting British universities and institutions working on COVID-19 research (Grierson and Devlin, 2020). In response to this and other attacks, the UK's Health Secretary gave the UK's intelligence service access and oversight to the NHS IT network in May 2020. In Table 11.1, the cyber resilience framework presented in Chapter 8 is applied to each of the healthcare organizations discussed in this chapter.

Table 11.1: *Healthcare organizations and the cyber resilience framework*

Event	Organize	Develop	Regulate	Connect
2017 WannaCry	Organizations should have a broader strategy rather than rely upon a series of tactical one-offs (Cooper, 2018).	The focus should not be on patching that vulnerability but having a reliable patching strategy. (Cooper, 2018)	Oversight of cyber should be at the Board and not the committee level (EIU, 2018)	77 percent of respondents to the 2018 Ponemon Institute study found they do not have a formal incident response plan (Ponemon, 2018)
2018 Norway Regional Health Authority Breach	The Health Authority had not implemented a strategy for responding to and adapting to attacks at the time of the breach (Irwin, 2018)	The attack took place before they could implement security measures (Irwin, 2018)	The GDPR regulations governing privacy protection were not followed (Warwick, 2018)	The Authority had not developed a warning system both before and after the attack to connect with authorities and private security that might have been helpful.
2020 Blackbaud	Lack of a strategy for ransomware caused a vendor of healthcare clients to pay ransom without confirmation that the copy they removed had been destroyed (Davis, 2020)	The major cause was unreasonable lack of oversight and security measures (Schwartz, 2020)	Facilitating ransomware payments on behalf of a victim may violate OFAC regulations if the criminal organization or individual is sanctioned or from a sanctioned jurisdiction (U.S. Treasury, 2020 Advisory)	There was no central reporting authority that would have made knowledge of the breach available much sooner or allowed faster notification to its victims (Schwartz, 2020).

11.4. WannaCry

In February 2021, the Department of Justice announced a federal indictment charging three North Korean computer programmers with participating in a wide-ranging criminal conspiracy to conduct a series of destructive cyberattacks, to steal and extort more than $1.3 billion of money and cryptocurrency from financial institutions and companies, to create and deploy multiple malicious cryptocurrency applications, and to develop and fraudulently market a blockchain platform (DOJ, 2021). These charges include Ransomware and Cyber-Enabled Extortion charges for the Creation of the destructive WannaCry 2.0 ransomware in May 2017, and the extortion and attempted extortion of victim companies from 2017 through 2020 involving the theft of sensitive data and deployment of the ransomware.

Since the WannaCry attack wreaked havoc across the world, the malware continued to impact devices with 40 percent of healthcare organizations suffering a WannaCry attack for three years just prior to the indictment. WannaCry is a ransomware cryptoworm that struck on May 12, 2017, infecting 300,000 computers globally in just a few short days. The hackers leveraged the EternalBlue exploit developed by the NSA, leaked a few months before the attack. While Microsoft released a patch for vulnerable systems months before the attack, many organizations did not apply it (Cooper, 2018). As a result, the exploit allowed the virus to proliferate, claiming the UK National Health Service as one of the hardest hit victims. The WannaCry attack could have done even more damage had a researcher not found a kill switch that prevented the malware from spreading, which stopped the cyberattack in four days. However, the kill switch did not eradicate the virus. The researchers noted that WannaCry was reportedly behind 30 percent of all ransomware attacks during the third quarter of 2018. Further, there were devices infected by WannaCry that weren't addressed during the attack, which continued its spread to other computers. *"Devices on which WannaCry did not activate are vulnerable to other attacks, as the ransomware's backdoor, Double Pulsar, remains wide open,"* Ben Seri, Armis vice president of research wrote. *"Many organizations fail to patch their networks, so any new variant of the ransomware, some of which lack a kill switch altogether, can compromise their security in an unstoppable attack"* (Davis, 2019).

Although not directly targeted, one of the biggest causalities of this WannaCry attack was the National Health Service (NHS) in England. Over 600 organizations were affected; this included 34 infected hospital trusts (NHS organizations that provide acute care, specialized medical services, mental healthcare, or ambulance services) and 46 affected hospital trusts (NAO, 2017). A report published by the Department of Health and Social Care (DHSC) has estimated that the cost to the NHS during the attack suggests the cyber-attack cost the service £20m during the outbreak and an additional £72m in the aftermath. because of lost output and a further £0.5m for additional IT support (DHSC, 2018). The DHSC's estimate was based on an anticipation that WannaCry would disrupt 1% of all NHS services including primary care (Ghafur et al., 2019). Reinforcing the need for cyber resilient strategies, the NAO report stated that none of the organizations affected by WannaCry had followed advice by NHS Digital (the national information and technology partner to the health and social care system) to apply a Microsoft update patch, which resulted in the vulnerability being exposed. This highlights the legacy systems and infrastructure that are in use, and since the WannaCry attack, funding has been made available for NHS organizations to upgrade their software to Microsoft Windows 10 to improve resilience. As highlighted in the cyber resilience framework, resilience comes not just from tactical compliance, but also raises the issue of education, awareness, and sharing of information to ensure that good practice can be developed and spread. To prevent or mitigate these types of events from recurring in the National Health Systems or in any other healthcare organization, there is a need to develop and test effective incident management procedures and improve business continuity planning (Sittig and Singh, 2016). All organizations must be able to safely and effectively function while under cyberattack. Meanwhile, all data and systems must be securely backed-up and disaster recovery processes tested to ensure that the backup is isolated and cannot be erased or tampered with (Ghafur, 2019). Strong leadership and a security culture throughout the healthcare sector can help significantly to improve patient safety.

11.5. Blackbaud 2020 Breach

The largest healthcare data breach of 2020 was a ransomware attack on the cloud service provider Blackbaud Inc which provides services to a range of nonprofits, healthcare systems, and hospitals (Davis, 2020). The actual number of records exposed and obtained by the hackers has not been made public, but more than 100 of Blackbaud's healthcare clients were affected and more than 10 million records are known to have been compromised. The 2020 Blackbaud incident is one of the best examples of just how great an impact a seemingly simple breach can have when it impacts a vendor. Much worse, the vendors paid the ransom demand "*without confirmation that the copy they removed had been destroyed.*" The breach does not appear on the OCR breach portal, as each entity affected has reported the breach separately. Prior to deploying ransomware, the hackers stole the fundraising and donor databases of many of its clients which included information such as names, contact information, dates of birth, and some clinical information. Victims included Trinity Health (3.3 million records), Inova Health System (1 million records), and Northern Light Health Foundation (657,392 records) (HIPPA Journal, 2021).

In response to the attack, at least 10 separate class-actions lawsuits were filed against Blackbaud, including in the US District Court of South Carolina in Charleston, US District Court Western District of Washington, and the California Central District Court (Davis, 2020). The victims alleged Blackbaud was negligent and breached its contract and that individuals are now at a heightened risk of identity theft and fraud. Another lawsuit argues that Blackbaud demonstrated an "*unreasonable lack of oversight and lax security measures.*" Blackbaud is also accused of failing to timely notify breach victims of the incident and its impact, as well as "*failing to properly monitor the computer network and systems that housed the private Information; failing to implement appropriate policies; and failing to properly train employees regarding cyberattacks.*"

"*Had Defendants properly monitored their networks, security, and communications, they would have prevented the data breach or would have discovered it sooner,*" according to the lawsuit filed in the District of Washington. The threats targeting healthcare continue to increase in both their frequency and sophistication. The need for developing a cyber resilient vendor management process will be crucial to reducing risks to the enterprise.

This case demonstrates the need for a framework that promotes resilience in organizational structure, leadership, oversight and compliance with regulations and connectivity with its numerous stakeholders including most importantly its customers.

11.6. Norway Regional Health Authority Breach

The South-Eastern Norway Regional Health Authority (South-East RHF) is a state-run region-specific organization of specialist hospitals and healthcare services created in 2002 alongside three other regional authorities. In January 2018, South-East RHF announced that the PHI and records of nearly 2.9 million people (more than half of the population of Norway) had been compromised (Khandelwal, 2018). It is suspected that a sophisticated criminal group from a foreign spy or state agency led the attack targeting both patient health data and the health service's interaction with Norway's armed forces (Hughes, 2018). While this attack did not seem to pose risks to patient safety or delays in hospital operations, the event raised concerns about future attacks on health data for the purpose of political gain and served as a wake-up call for GDPR. Under GDPR, the organization would have had to notify those affected within 72 h, which it did not do (Warwick, 2018).

On 30 January 2019 Norway published its 4th National Cyber Security Strategy with an implementation budget of 1.6B NOK. Though resilience is not a term used in the strategy it does promote many of the features of a strong resilience framework. These include improved competence both within and outside government institutions, a strong emphasis on collaboration between the public and private sector, a focus on prevention and detection and combatting cyber-crime and the promotion of international cooperation and partnerships (Norway, 2019).

11.7. Emerging Cyber Issues in the Health Care Industry

11.7.1. The Risk of Shared Data in Healthcare

In recent years cyber-attacks in the health care industry and in hospitals has been rampant. On September 9, 2015, Excellus Health Plan filed a breach report stating that cyber-attackers had gained unauthorized access to its information technology systems. Excellus Health Plan reported that the breach began on or before December 23, 2013 and ended on May 11, 2015. The hackers installed malware and conducted reconnaissance activities that ultimately resulted in the impermissible disclosure of the protected health information of more than 9.3 million individuals, including their names, addresses, dates of birth, email addresses, Social Security numbers, bank account information, health plan claims, and clinical treatment information. OCR's investigation found potential violations of the HIPAA Rules including failure to conduct an enterprise-wide risk analysis, and failures to implement risk management, information system activity review, and access controls. On January 2021, the U.S. Department of Health and Human Services reported that Excellus Health Plan, Inc. had agreed to pay $5.1 million to the Office for Civil Rights (OCR) at the U.S. Department of Health and Human Services (HHS) and to implement a corrective action plan to settle potential violations of the Health Insurance Portability and Accountability Act (HIPAA) (HHS, 2021).

A healthcare and cyber security review by KPMG showed that among the greatest vulnerabilities in data security is sharing data between third parties and insiders (breaches by employees) (KPMG, 2015). This finding indicates access control and authentication as key security features in eHealth infrastructures. Authentication is the initial stage of the users' validation in order to determine their identity which is necessary to ensure that they are authorized to access the system. Once authenticated, the information level that they are allowed to view or share for organizational purposes is defined by an access control policy. Access control is one of the main safeguards for ensuring data privacy and integrity. A centralized system (Health Information System) with limited external connection has a specific perimeter which needs to be safeguarded. In such a case, internal user access control becomes a higher challenge than external access control. In the past, hospitals experienced difficulties with devices that refuse operating system patches or that became functionally compromised when, for example, Microsoft Windows was updated multiple times (Quatris Health, 2016). Consequently, hospitals had to delay or refrain from closing various security gaps in the operating system. There has been a recent push to promote cyber resilience as a value proposition among medical device and equipment manufacturers, shifting the approach to cyber resilience by motivating them to value it and sell it as an asset (Tanev and Apiafi, 2015). Cyber resilience is not simply plugged in as an afterthought but has become one of the prerequisites of the design (Alvarenga and Tanev, 2017). This has also been reinforced by the US Food and Drug Administration (FDA), that expects manufacturers to implement on-going lifecycle processes and to monitor continued safety post-market (FDA, 2020). Recently, the Food and Drug Administration has released guidelines on communicating to patients the risks of cyber vulnerabilities (FDA, 2020).

In 2017, the FDA began mandating that medical device manufacturers show that their devices are able to have updates and security patches applied throughout their lifespan. Additionally, they must show that they have addressed any undesirable issues that would affect the patients if the device were to be compromised. As part of this same regulation, the FDA requires that a "bill of materials" be shared with buyers of a medical device. The bill of materials provides transparency to the device buyer as to the source of each component (hardware and software) contained in the medical device. These new rules will apply to manufacturers, who must submit a 510(k)-pre-market submission package to the FDA (FDA, 2017). These measures put the onus on manufacturers, however, the call to approach cybersecurity with a more engaged and proactive stance should not be limited to manufacturers but should challenge health facilities as well. Hospitals ought to invest in prevention by designating resources and budgeting early, rather than depending on reactive approaches following attacks; this might be difficult in light of historic underinvestment in human resources. Information sharing between stakeholders is also recommended in order to build resilience.

11.7.2. Cyber Resilience and COVID 19

The Coronavirus Disease 2019 (COVID-19) pandemic has resulted in widespread disruption to the healthcare industry. Alongside complex issues relating to ensuring sufficient healthcare capacity and resourcing, healthcare organizations and universities are now also facing heightened cybersecurity threats in the midst of the pandemic. Since the outbreak began, various healthcare providers and academic institutions across the world have been targeted in a variety of complex and coordinated cyber-attacks. International and national regulatory bodies have stressed the urgent need for healthcare providers and universities to protect themselves against cyber-attacks during COVID-19, recognizing that a growing number of cyber-criminals are seeking to capitalize on the vulnerabilities of the healthcare sector during this period. This includes a desire to steal intellectual property such as data relating to COVID-19 vaccine development, modelling and experimental therapeutics. It is therefore essential that healthcare providers and universities ensure they are informed, protected, and prepared to respond to any cyber-threat (Muthuppalaniappan and Stevenson, 2020).

One of the early attacks on the health care industry during COVID 19 was reported on 13 March 2020 at the Brno University Hospital, Czech Republic, one of the Czech Republic's biggest COVID-19 testing laboratories (Cimpanu, 2020). The attack involved the shut-down of the IT network that caused postponement of urgent surgeries and compromised emergency medical care. On the same day, the World Health Organization reported the creation of a malicious site mimicking the WHO internal email system which aimed to steal employee passwords. A few days later in the U.S. the Health and Human Services (HHS) Department reported an unspecified attack on the HHS servers. These attacks have continued relentlessly on the global health care industry, and it is likely that the cure for the COVID virus will be resolved long before the cyber virus is ever resolved.

In June 2020, hackers infiltrated servers in the epidemiology and biostatistics department of the University of California at San Francisco. The attack could not have come at a worse time since the department was racing to develop the COVID-19 vaccine. Reports indicate that it took a weeklong negotiation to free its ransomware-locked servers. According to a July 2020 U.S. Department of Justice indictment, Chinese MSS-affiliated actors have targeted various industries across the United States and other countries and recently probed for vulnerabilities in computer networks of companies developing COVID-19 vaccines, testing technology, and treatments (DOJ, 2020a). In the U.K., the National Cyber Security Centre documented a surge in state-sponsored attacks on British research institutions focused on COVID-19, and attributed much of that increase to Russia, Iran, and China (Bloomberg, 2020; Khare, 2020).

In Europe, The COVID-19 pandemic underlined an increased need for efficient – and secure – digital healthcare services. Cloud solutions has been offered to address the need for rapid deployment of the electronic storage of data and electronic communications such as telemedicine. However, the complexity of legal systems and new technologies, as well as concerns over the security of sensitive patient data slowed the healthcare sector in adopting cloud services. To expedite the process on January 18, 2021, the European Union Agency for Cybersecurity (ENISA) published the Cloud Security for Healthcare Services report, which provides cybersecurity guidelines for healthcare organizations to help further digitalize with cloud services. Building on ENISA's 2020 procurement guidelines for cybersecurity in hospitals, this latest report assesses the cybersecurity risks of cloud services and offers good practices for their secure integration into the European healthcare sector. Simultaneously, the European Commission moved forward with the European Health Data Space initiative to promote the safe exchange of patients' data and access to health data (EC, 2021b). The initiative is set up to help the Members States and the Commission facilitate the sharing of health data for public health, treatment, research, and innovation in Europe. The European Health Data Space will be built on 3 main pillars: (1) a strong system of data governance and rules for data exchange; (2) data quality; and 3) strong infrastructure and interoperability. This is a good start for Europe but remains a challenge with each European country at different stages of maturity in terms of their implementation of security and resilience in eHealth (ENISA, 2021).

11.8. Summary

Since the healthcare industry is a life-or-death industry cyber resilience practices should take the highest priority. Healthcare institutions should be prepared to handle the short- and long-term impacts of any attack, bearing in mind the economic and legal implications, and must have robust business continuity plans in place. Alongside this, they should establish a 'security culture' amongst staff by ensuring cyber-security training for all employees (Muthuppalaniappan and Stevenson, 2020). All healthcare institutions including academic institutions should assess the risks presented by a cyber-attack in the COVID-19 context and develop a detailed plan for adaptation and recovery enlisting the support of government agencies, the private sector, and international cyber research institutions to build cyber operational resilience in all of their facilities, laboratories, and supply chains. Finally, what makes health care difficult when it comes to cyber resilience is balancing the safety of patients against security, privacy, and compliance with data protection regulations (Argaw et al., 2020). This requires a holistic approach to health care cyber resilience so that a collective, multidisciplinary team is involved in ensuring the highest standards of safety resilient practices.

Chapter 12

Conclusion: Moving Resilience Forward

Do not judge me by my success, judge me by how many times I fell down and got back up again.

Nelson Mandela

This book reviewed and compared cyber resilience frameworks at the transnational, national and local levels within both the public and private sectors. Various cyber resiliency standards have been proposed in the past, but none provides a broad perspective of the necessary components of cyber resilience on a global level. These standards to some extent serve different purposes and are particularly useful for stated purposes.

As we have described in this book cyber resilience requires going beyond the traditional passive activities of cyber security and risk management. We must stay way ahead of the cyber-attackers not only technologically but also through prioritizing cyber resilience as the most important value in our organizations both at the strategic and organizational level.

We presented a framework for cyber resilience based on real world cyber scenarios. Our recommendations address concerns about interoperability, strategy, regulation, connectivity, trade-offs between privacy and security, cultural differences, the digital divide, accountability, and political challenges in moving resilience forward (WEF, 2016). To implement this framework, we need to understand the cultural, behavioral, cross-sectoral, and leadership dimensions of resilience. This involves determining how leaders can incentivize teams to explore innovative ways of analyzing resilience and developing methodologies for encouraging divergent groups to develop the key attributes and capabilities for resilience.

12.1. Holistic Approaches for Cyber Resilience

12.1.1. Protection of the Cyber Ecosystem

According to ENISA, a framework or the development of an approach to cyber resilience requires a commitment, organization, coordination, and strategy (ENISA Threat Report, 2016). This could include (but not be restricted to) attack pattern recognition and knowledge discovery and enrichment of cyber-threat context. This should also include the use of cyber-threat intelligence and metrics to assess efficiency and performance of implemented security controls. Research in new innovative security controls considers that there is a need for development of trust between components but also users, and that it should be based not only on "something you know" and "something you possess", but also "something you are."

To do so, a more holistic approach to cyber resilience must include not only the technical aspects of identify, adapt, respond, and recover the physical infrastructure but more behavioral aspects as well that include cultural, cross-sectional leadership and respect for privacy and human rights. The foundation for a cyber resilient structure requires a bottom-up approach to resilience. This involves practices that encourage integration of the cyber resilience framework with cybersecurity and operational risk management frameworks discussed in the early chapters of this book. This requires not only intraorganizational resilience but interorganizational practices based on the network of alliances that are essential to achieve resilience. This is of particular importance in the banking, healthcare, and technology industries.

To be cyber resilient does not mean just meeting technological capabilities or compliance with detailed standards but is rooted more in social science and organizational change. As discussed in this book it involves learning and forward-thinking approaches including "reinvention." While much has been written about frameworks that address system domains, very little research has been conducted on the actual benefits cyber resilience brings in the broader sense. This book sought to distinguish cyber resilience from the narrower more passive focus on cyber security and risk management. Cyber resilience creates value not just through its attention to sustaining and being able to move forward in an institutional context but through its contribution in protecting the wider eco system.

12.2. Progressive Cyber Resilience

As discussed throughout this book, implementing a cyber resilience plan is not simple. It will impact the organization at every level and will require a significant human and financial investment. Even when all the conditions are met, and cyber security has reached a high level of maturity, and includes the systems of the supply chain stakeholders, achieving this transformation to resilience competency is complicated.

Most of the frameworks and methodologies focus on the operationalization of cyber resilience and propose a set of policies, very specific and at the same time similar regardless of the size of the company and the nature of its activity. Moreover, without a holistic vision of cyber resilience, it is difficult for companies to prioritize their actions. Getting into the process then seems too complicated and costly.

Recent research proposes a relevant approach to progressive cyber resilience that can be used as a guide for companies starting to operationalize cyber resilience, especially those lacking experience in that matter. The idea is to use a progression model that will allow companies to strategize and prioritize cyber resilience policies by proposing the natural evolution of the policies over time (Carías et al, 2020). The authors propose several progression models concerning operational aspects such as risk management policies, threat and vulnerability management policies, asset management policies, detection processes and continuous monitoring policies, information security policies or incident analysis policies. They also propose progression models to apprehend the more managerial aspects, such as governance policies, business continuity management policies, awareness and training policies, and information sharing and communication policies.

The first advantage of such an approach is that it helps companies to situate themselves quite easily, and then to define target situations. The second is that it de-dramatizes the concept by defining policies without technical jargon and shows "*how the essential cyber resilience policies manifest at their beginning stages and how they progress over time*" (Carías et al, 2020).

In any case, no company will be able to achieve a high level of cyber resilience maturity overnight. Because all the existing models are so comprehensive, using them can be difficult, especially for smaller companies. But these small businesses also manage data, which is poorly protected due to the lack of skills and resources in these organizations. They are all the more prey to cyber-attackers as security is easy to compromise. The problem is that these companies are numerous, and that together they represent millions of confidential records.

Using a framework that would allow them to take ownership of the concepts, and jointly develop their cyber security and cyber resilience may be a good strategy. But like any strategy, it will involve several implementation steps. It is in this respect that a progressive implementation makes sense.

12.3. Interconnected Cyber Resilience for an Interconnected World

Having a holistic vision of cyber resilience also requires that all relevant stakeholders be included in the thinking and implementation. Indeed, one is never stronger than one's weakest link. The effects of cyber security breaches on an entire supply chain can be numerous through a ripple effect. Moreover, the companies concerned may be small, and will not have had the financial capacity to protect themselves against risks.

Managing the cyber resilience of the supply chain is therefore a major challenge today. This could lead large organizations to ask themselves the same questions as when implementing inter-organizational systems on the approach to adopt: should they accompany their suppliers in an integration and cyber security approach? Should they rationalize their suppliers, and only use those certified by cyber security agencies to limit risks? In any case, this will require a financial and organizational investment.

The complexity will be increased by the fact that globalization means that many interconnected partners are located in different countries and are subject to different laws. The national and legal pressure will therefore be different, as will the regulations they must follow. There is therefore a need for greater international cooperation to define consistent and sustainable regulations for all organizations, regardless of their size or field of activity. The significant differences in data privacy between the US and Europe, however, show that the complexity of such an approach means that if it happens, it will not be for many years. The cultural divide is too strong. In the meantime, organizations can maximize their cyber resilience by encouraging cooperation with all their stakeholders, in order to bring about change gradually.

For these purposes, we have proposed a framework inspired by the Corporate and Social Responsibility (CSR) approach. In the same way, to be effective and sustainable, cyber resilience must be initiated by top management, and carried out on a daily basis by employees. This change in organizational culture can only be achieved gradually, which also argues in favor of a gradual implementation. Like CSR, the optimum level of cyber resilience will be reached the day organizations no longer need to make specific plans to implement it. This will mean that it is ingrained in organizational and individual behaviors in the normal course of every-day life. If we wanted to sum it up in one sentence: cyber resilience will be achieved the day, it is so natural that we no longer talk about it! Until then, Cyber Resilience remains a global challenge.

References

Abraham, C. and Sims, R.R. (2021, March 13). A Comprehensive Approach to Cyber Resilience. *MIT Sloan Manag Rev*. Massachusetts Institute of Technology, Cambridge.

Allen, S. (2020) Deloitte Insights: 2020 Global Health Care Outlook. https://www2.deloitte.com/content/dam/Deloitte/cz/Documents/life-sciences-health-care/2020-global-health-care-outlook.pdf.

Alvarenga A, and Tanev G. (2017) Cybersecurity risk assessment framework that integrates value-sensitive design. *Technol Innov Manag Rev.* Vol. 7, 32–43.

Aon. (2020, December 31) Bangladesh Bank Heist: Lessons in Cyber Vulnerability. Aon, New, York.

Applegate, S.C. and Stavrou, A. (2013) Towards a Cyber Conflict Taxonomy. 5th International Conference on Cyber Conflict, NATO CCD COE, Tallinn.

Argaw, S.T., Troncoso-Pastoriza, J.R., Lacey, D. et al. (2020) Cybersecurity of Hospitals: Discussing the challenges and working towards mitigating the risks. *BMC Med Inform Decis Mak* vol 20, 146. https://doi.org/10.1186/s12911-020-01161-7.

Australia Government (2020) *Australia's Cyber Security Strategy* 2020. https://www.homeaffairs.gov.au/cyber-security-subsite/files/cyber-security-strategy-2020.pdf.

Austrian Government (2013) *Austrian National Cyber Security Strategy* (NCCS). https://www.bmi.gv.at/504/files/130415_strategie_cybersicherheit_en_web.pdf.

BaFin Federal Financial Supervisory Authority (2020) *Perspective,* Issue 1, Cyber Security. Bonn and Frankfurt, Germany.

BaFin Federal Financial Supervisory Authority (2021, February 14) Focus on Cyber Resilience. Bonn and Frankfurt, Germany.

Bagheri, S. and Ridley, G. (2017, December) Organizational cyber resilience: Research opportunities. 28th Australasian Conference on Information Systems.

Bank for International Settlements (BIS) (2016) Guidance on cyber resilience for financial market infrastructures. Bank for International Settlements, Committee on Payments and Market Infrastructures, Board of the International Organization of Securities Commissions, June.

Bank for International Settlements (BIS) (2020) Basel Committee on Banking Supervision Consultative Document. Revisions to the principles for the sound management of operational risk.

Bank of England (BoE, 2016). *CBEST Intelligence-Led Testing: Understanding Cyber Threat Intelligence Operations,* Version 2.0.

Bank of England (BoE, 2019), Prudential Regulation Authority (PRA) and Financial Conduct Authority (FCA). Building the UK financial sector's operational resilience.

Bargar, A. (2009) Cyber Resilience for Mission Assurance. Unrestricted Warfare Symposium Proceedings on Combating the Unrestricted Warfare Threat: Terrorism, Resources, Economics, and Cyberspace 24-25 March. John Hopkins University. https://www.jhuapl.edu/Content/documents/2009-URW.pdf.

Barlow, J. P. (1996) *A Declaration of the Independence of Cyberspace*. Davos, Switzerland, February 8.

Benson M. H., and Craig R. K. (2014) The end of sustainability. *Society and Natural Resources*, Vol. 27 (7) 777–82.

Bertels, S., Papania, L., Papania, D. (2010) Embedding sustainability in organizational culture. Network for Business Sustainability.

Bishop, M. (1995) *A Taxonomy of UNIX System and Network Vulnerabilities.* University of California at Davis. Report CSE-95-10.

Björck F., Henkel M., Stirna J., Zdravkovic J. (2015) Cyber Resilience – Fundamentals for a Definition. In: Rocha A., Correia A., Costanzo S., Reis L. (eds) *New Contributions in Information Systems and Technologies. Advances in Intelligent Systems and Computing,* vol 353. Springer, Cham. https://doi.org/10.1007/978-3-319-16486-1_31.

Blankertz, A. and Jaursch, J. (2020) How the EU plans to rewrite the rules for the Internet. Brookings Tech Stream, 21 October. https://www.brookings.edu/techstream/how-the-eu-plans-to-rewrite-the-rules-for-the-internet/.

Bloomberg (2020) How Hackers Bled 118 Bitcoins out of Covid Researchers in U.S, August 19. https://www.bloomberg.com/news/features/2020-08-19/ucsf-hack-shows-evolving-risks-of-ransomware-in-the-covid-era.

Borst, W. (1997) Construction of Engineering Ontologies. PhD thesis, Institute for Telematica and Information Technology, University of Twente, Enschede, The Netherlands.

Boston Consulting Group (BCG) (2019) Global Wealth 2019: Reigniting Radical Growth. BCG, Boston.

Canada Office of the Privacy Commissioner (Canada, 2019) Investigation into Equifax Inc. And Equifax Canada Co.'s compliance with PIPEDA in light of the 2017 breach of personal information. The Personal Information Protection and Electronic Documents Act (PIPEDA) Report of Findings #2019-001, April.

Carías, J.E., Arrizabalaga, S., Labaka, L., Hernantes, J. (2020) Cyber Resilience Progression Model, *Applied Science*, vol. *10* (21), 7393; https://doi.org/10.3390/app10217393.

Carnegie Mellon University (2016) CERT Resilience Management Model, Version 1.2, February.

Cebula, J. J., and Lisa, R. Y. (2010) *A Taxonomy of Operational Cyber Security Risks.* Carnegie Mellon University Software Engineering Institute No. CMU/SEI-2010- TN-028.

Center for Strategic and International Studies (CSIS) (2017) *From Awareness to Action: A Cybersecurity Agenda for the 45th President, A report of the CSIS Policy Task Force*, The Center for Strategic and International Studies, Washington, D.C., January.

Checkpoint Software Technology (CST) (2021) Attacks targeting healthcare organizations spike globally as COVID-19 cases rise again. https://blog.checkpoint.com/2021/01/05/attacks-targeting-healthcare-organizations-spike-globally-as-covid-19-cases-rise-again/.

Chin, J. and Dou, E. (2016) China's New Cybersecurity Law Rattles Foreign Tech Firms. The Wall Street Journal, November 7.

China. (2017) *The Draft Information Security Technology - Guidelines for Data Cross-Border Transfer Security Assessment.* The National Information Security Standardization Technical Committee of China (TC260).

Chmutina, K., Bosher, L., Coaffee, J., & Rowlands, R. (2014) Procedia *Economics and Finance,* vol. 18, 25–32. https://doi.org/10.1016/S2212-5671(14)0 Towards Integrated Security and Resilience Framework: A Tool for Decision-makers. 0909-5.

Christopher, M. (2011) *Logistics and Supply Chain Management* (4th ed.). London: FT Prentice Hall.

Christou, G. (2016) *Cyber security in the European Union: resilience and adaptability in governance policy*. Palgrave Macmillan, Basingstoke, UK.

Cimpanu, C. (2020, March 13) Czech hospital hit by cyberattack while in the midst of a COVID-19 outbreak. https://www.zdnet.com/article/czech-hospital-hit-by-cyber-attack-while-in-the-midst-of-a-covid-19-outbreak/.

References

Commin, G. and Filiol E. (2015) Unrestricted Warfare versus Western Traditional Warfare: A Comparative Study in J. Ryan (ed). *Leading Issues in Cyber Warfare and Security*, vol. 2, 82. Academic Conferences and Publishing International Lmtd., Reading, England. Originally published in the proceedings of ECIW, 2013.

Conklin, W., Shoemaker, D., & Kohnke, A. (2017). Cyber Resilience: Rethinking Cybersecurity Strategy to Build a Cyber Resilient Architecture. Proceedings of the 12th International Conference on Cyber Warfare and Security.

Constantin, L. (2020, December 15) SolarWinds attack explained: And why it was so hard to detect, IDG Communications. https://www.solar winds attack.

Convention on Cybercrime of the Council of Europe (CETS No.185), known as the Budapest Convention. Open for signature on 23 November 2001.

Cooper, C. (2018, May 15) WannaCry- Lessons Learned 1 Year Later. WannaCry demonstrated the destructive potential of ransomware, which remains as dangerous as ever. Broadcom, Symantic Enterprise Blogs.

Council of the European Union (CDPF, 2018) *EU Cyber Defence Policy Framework* (2018 Update) 14413/18. General Secretariat of the Council, Brussels 19 November 2018.

Critical Infrastructure Information Protection Law (CIIP, 2013), December 18. France.

Crowdstrike (2021) *Global Threat Report.* https://go.crowdstrike.com/rs/281-OBQ-266/images/Report2021GTR.pdf.

Cyber Export Group (2019) G7 fundamental elements of cybersecurity for the financial sector. https://www.banque-france.fr/sites/default/files/media/2019/03/08/g7_fundamental_elements_oct_2016_0.pdf.

Cyber Infrastructure and Security Agency (CISA) (2020) *Cybersecurity and Infrastructure Frameworks.* https://us-cert.cisa.gov/resources/cybersecurity-framework.

Cybersecurity Information Sharing Act (CISA) (2015) Pub. L. No. 114-113S. 2588 [113th Congress], S. 754 [114th Congress].

Cybersecurity Tech Accord (CTA) The 2020 Year In Review. (2021) https://cybertechaccord.org/uploads/prod/2021/05/tech-accord-2021-annual-report-pages-050521.pdf.

Das, K.N. and Spicer, J. (2016, July 21) The Swift Hack: How the New York Fed fumbled over the Bangladesh Bank cyber-heist, Reuters. https://www.reuters.com/investigates/special-report/cyber-heist-federal/.

Daugirdas, K. and Mortenson, J.D. (2015) Contemporary Practice of the United States relating to International Law, 109 *AJIL* 644, 649.

Davis, A. (2015) Building Cyber Resilience into Supply Chains. *Technology Innovation Management Review,* April.

Davis, J. (2019, May 30) 40% of Health Organizations Suffered WannaCry Attack in Past 6 Months. Health IT Security. Xtelligent Healthcare Media.

Davis, J. (2020) Blackbaud Confirms Hackers Stole Some SSNs, as Lawsuits Increase. Health IT Security. Xtelligent Healthcare Media. https://healthitsecurity.com/news/blackbaud-confirms-hackers-stole-some-ssns-as-lawsuits-increase.

Denmark (2018) *Danish Cyber and Information Security Strategy 2018-2021.* Agency for Digitisation, Ministry of Finance, Denmark.

Department of Defense (DoD, 2015) *Cybersecurity Culture and Compliance Initiative* (DC 3I) (2015 September 30). Office of the Secretary of Defense, Washington, D.C.

Department of Defense *Law of War Manual* (DoD, 2016). Office of General Counsel, Department of Defense, Washington, D.C.

Department of Defense (DoD) (2017) Joint and National Intelligence Support to Military Operations, Washington, D.C., 5 July

Department of Defense (DoD) (2018a) *Cyber Strategy.* Office of the Secretary of Defense, Washington, D.C.

Department of Defense (DoD) (2018b) *Summary of the National Defense Strategy of the United States of America: Sharpening the American Military's Competitive* Edge. Office of the Secretary of Defense, Washington, D.C.

Department of Defense Joint Operations. (2018) (DoD, JP 3.0) incorporating change 1, 22 October 2018. Office of the Director for Joint Force Development, Washington, D.C.

Department of Defense Joint Planning (2020, December 1) JP 5-0, xx-xxi. Office of the Director for Joint Force Development, Washington, D.C.

Department of Defense (DoD) (2020, June 1) *Strategic Cyberspace Operations Guide.* Center for Strategic Leadership. U.S. Army War College, U.S. Department of Defense.

Department of Defense Science Board (DSB, 2017) *Final Report of the Task Force on Cyber Deterrence,* Office of the Under Secretary of Defense for Acquisition, Technology, and Logistics, Washington, D.C., February.

Department of Health and Social Care (DHSC) (2018). *Securing cyber resilience in health and care.* https://assets.publishing.service.gov.uk/government/uploads/system/uploads/attachment_data/file/747464/securing-cyber-resilience-in-health-and-care-september-2018-update.pdf.

Department of Homeland Security (DHS, 2014) *Quadrennial Homeland Security Review* (QHSR). DHS, Washington, D.C. estayhttps://www.dhs.gov/sites/default/files/publications/2014-qhsr-final-508.pdf.

Department of Homeland Security (DHS, 2018) Cyber Resilience and Response 2018 Public-Private Analytic Exchange Program. DHS, Washington, D.C. https://www.dhs.gov/sites/default/files/publications/2018_AEP_Cyber_Resilience_and_Response.pdf.

Department of Homeland Security (DHS, 2019) *Annual Performance Report*. March 18, DHS, Washington, D.C. https://www.dhs.gov/sites/default/files/publications/19_0318_MGMT_APR-FY-2018-2020.pdf.

Department of Homeland Security (DHS, 2020) *Cyber Resilience Review (CRR) Method Description and Self-Assessment User Guide*. U.S. Department of Homeland Security Cybersecurity and Infrastructure Security Agency (CISA), April. https://us-cert.cisa.gov/sites/default/files/c3vp/csc-crr-method-description-and-user-guide.pdf.

Department of Justice (DOJ, 2018) Thirty-six Defendants Indicted for Alleged Roles in Transnational Criminal Organization Responsible for More than $530 Million in Losses from Cybercrimes. February 7. https://www.justice.gov/opa/pr/thirty-six-defendants-indicted-alleged-roles-transnational-criminal-organization-responsible.

Department of Justice (DOJ, 2020a) Two Chinese Hackers Working with the Ministry of State Security Charged with Global Computer Intrusion Campaign Targeting Intellectual Property and Confidential Business Information, Including COVID-19 Research. DOJ, Office of Public Affairs. July 21.

https://www.justice.gov/opa/pr/two-chinese-hackers-working-ministry-state-security-charged-global-computer-intrusion.

Department of Justice (DOJ, 2020b) Six Russian GRU Officers Charged in Connection with Worldwide Deployment of Destructive Malware and Other Disruptive Actions in Cyberspace, DOJ, Office of Public Affairs, October 19. https://www.justice.gov/opa/pr/six-russian-gru-officers-charged-connection-worldwide-deployment-destructive-malware-and

Department of Justice (DOD, 2020c) Chinese Military Personnel Charged with Computer Fraud, Economic Espionage and Wire Fraud for Hacking into Credit Reporting Agency Equifax. DOJ, Office of Public Affairs, February 10. https://www.justice.gov/opa/pr/chinese-military-personnel-charged-computer-fraud-economic-espionage-and-wire-fraud-hacking.

Department of Justice (DOJ, 2021) Three North Korean Military Hackers Indicted in Wide-Ranging Scheme to Commit Cyberattacks and Financial Crimes Across the Globe. DOJ, Office of Public Affairs. February 17.

References

Duarte de Jesus, C. (2017) Le cyberespace : quelle coopération au sein de l'Union Euro-péenne? https://www.eyes-on-europe.eu/cyberespace-cooperation-sein-de-lunion-europeenne/.

Dunn Cavelty, M. and Prior, T. (2013) *Resiliency in Security Policy: Present and Future.* Center for Security Studies, Zurich, Switzerland.

Dupont, B. (2019) The cyber-resilience of financial institutions: Significance and applicabil-ity, *Journal of Cybersecurity*, 2019, 1–17, doi: 10.1093/cybsec/tyz013.

Economist Intelligence Unit (EIU, 2019) (2019, September 29) *World Industry Outlook: Healthcare and Pharmaceuticals.* The Economist Group.

E-ISAC. (2016) *Analysis of the Cyber-attack on the Ukranian Power Grid: Defense Use Case.* Electricity Information Sharing and Analysis Center (E-ISAC) and Sans In-dustrial Control Systems, March 18.

Estay, D. A. S., Sahay, R., Barfod, M.B., Jensen, C.D. (2020) A systematic review of cyber-resilience assessment frameworks, *Computer & Security* 97.

Estonia (ENCP), National Cyber Security in Practice (2020) e-Governance Academy, Tal-linn.

European Central Bank (ECB, 2018) Cyber resilience oversight expectations for financial market infrastructures, December. https://www.ecb.europa.eu/paym/pdf/cons/cyber-resilience/Cyber_resilience_oversight_expectations_for_financial_market_infra-structures.pdf.

European Commission, (EC, 2017a). *Resilience, Deterrence and Defence: Building strong cybersecurity for the EU*. High Representative of the Union for Foreign Affairs and Security Policy, Joint Communication to the European Parliament and the Council, Brussels, September 9.

European Commission (EC, 2017b) *Commission Recommendation on Coordinated Re-sponse to Large Scale Cybersecurity Incidents and Crises and Blueprint for Coordi-nated response to large-scale cross-border cybersecurity incidents and crises.* Euro-pean Commission, Brussels.

European Commission (EC, 2017c) *From Shared Vision to Common Action: Implementing the EU Global Strategy Year 1: A Global Strategy for the European Union's For-eign and Security Policy*. Brussels.

European Commission. (EC) 2019) Digital Operational Resilience Framework for financial services: Making the EU financial sector more secure. *European Union Cyber Secu-rity Strategy*. Brussels.

European Commission (EC) (2020a), *New EU Cybersecurity Strategy and new rules to make physical and digital critical entities more resilient.* https://ec.europa.eu/com-mission/presscorner/detail/en/IP_20_2391.

European Commission. (EC) (2020b) Digital Finance Package: Commission Sets Out New, Ambitious Approach to Encourage Responsible Innovation to Benefit Consumers and Businesses. European Commission, Brussels, September 24. https://ec.eu-ropa.eu/commission/presscorner/detail/en/ IP_20_1684.

European Commission, (EC) (2021a) The Directive on security of network and information systems (the NIS Directive), 26 March.

European Commission. (EC) (2021b) European Health Data Space, Brussels.

European Economic and Social Committee (EESC, 2018) Cybersecurity: Ensuring aware-ness and resilience of the private sector across Europe in face of mounting cyber risks, The Hague Centre for Strategic Studies.

European External Action Service (EEAS) (2019), https://eeas.europa.eu/.

European Network and Information Security Agency (ENISA) (2011a) *Ontologies and Tax-onomies of Resilience, version 1.0.* (eds.) Vlacheas, P.T., Stavroulaki, V., Cadzow, S., Gorniak, S., Idonomou, D. European Network and Information Security Agency (ENISA).

European Network and Information Security Agency (ENISA) (2011b) *Measurement Frameworks and Metrics for Resilient Networks and Services: Challenges and Recommendations.* https://www.enisa.europa.eu/publications/metrics-tech-report/at_download/fullReport.

European Network and Information Security Agency (ENISA) (2015) *Security and Resilience in eHealth Infrastructures and Services.*

European Network and Information Security Agency (ENISA) (2016a) *NCSS Good Practice Guide: Designing and Implementing National Cyber Security Strategies.*

European Network and Information Security Agency (ENISA) (2016b) *Threat Landscape Report.*

European Network and Information Security Agency (ENISA, 2018) *Recommendations on shaping technology according to GDPR provisions an overview on data pseudonymization.* November. https://www.anonos.com/hubfs/ENISA_Pseudonymisation_Recomendations_GDPR_November_2018.pdf.

European Network and Information Security Agency (ENISA) (2020) *Ransomware: ENISA Threat Landscape Overview from January 2019 – April 2020.*

European Network and Information Security Agency (ENISA) (2021) *Cloud Security for Healthcare Services.* https://www.enisa.europa.eu/publications/cloud-security-for-healthcare-services.

European Parliament resolution of 13 June 2018 on cyber defence (2018/2004(INI).

European Union General Data Protection Regulation (EU GDPR, 2016) 2016/679 of the European Parliament and of the Council of the European Union, and the European Commission 27 April 2016 on the protection of natural persons with regard to the processing of persona l data and on the free movement of such data and repealing Directive 95/46/EC (General Data Protection Regulation).

European Union Regulation (EU) (2019) (EU) 2019/881 of the European Parliament and of the Council on ENISA (the European Union Agency for Cybersecurity) and on information and communications technology cybersecurity certification.

Federal Bureau of Investigation. (2021, May 9) Statement on Compromise of Colonial Pipeline Networks, FBI National Press Office, Washington, D.C.

Federal Financial Institutions Examination Council (FFIEC) (2017) Cybersecurity Assessment Tool. https://www.ffiec.gov/cyberassessmenttool.htm.

Federal Food and Drug Administration (FDA, 2017) *Medical Device Safety Action Plan.* Silver Spring: FDA; 2018. 1-18. 2017 HIMSS Cybersecurity survey. Chicago: HIMSS; 2017. pp. 5–37.

Federal Food and Drug Administration (FDA, 2020). *Communicating Cybersecurity Vulnerabilities to Patients: Considerations for a Framework.* FDA, Washington, D.C.

Federal Reserve Bank (FRB) (2020, October 30) Agencies release paper on operational resilience. Board of Governors of the Federal Reserve System. https://www.federalreserve.gov/newsevents/pressreleases/bcreg20201030a.htm.

Financial Stability Board, (FSB) (2020) *Effective Practices for Cyber Incident Response and Recover: Consultative document.* https://www.fsb.org/2020/04/effectivepractices-for-cyber-incident-response-and-recovery-consultative-document/.

Finkle, J. and Quadir, S. (2016, March 20) SWIFT to advise banks on security as Bangladesh hack details emerge. Technology Newsmarch.

Finklea, K., Christensen, M.D., Fischer, E.A., Lawrence, S.V., Theohary, C.A. (2015, July 17) Cyber Intrusion into U.S. Office of Personnel Management: In Brief. Congressional Research Service (CRS) 7-5700, Washington, D.C.

Fischer, E. A., Liu, E.C., Rollins, J. W. and Theohary, C.A. (2014, December 15) The 2013 Cybersecurity Executive Order: Overview and Considerations for Congress, Congressional Research Service Report, Washington, D.C.

References

Fleron, B., Pries-Heje, J., Baskerville, R. (2021) Digital Organizational Resilience: A History of Denmark as a Most Digitalized Country. Proceedings of the 54th Hawaii International Conference on System Sciences, pp. 2400-2409.

Fovino, I. N., Coletta, A., Masera, M., (2010) *Taxonomy of security solutions for the SCADA Sector, Deliverable: D 2.2, Version: 1.1.* A European Network for The Security of Control and Real Time Systems, March.

France 24 (2021), France uncovers cybersecurity breaches linked to Russian hackers, 02/16/21, https://www.france24.com/en/france/20210216-france-uncovers-cybersecurity-breaches-linked-to-russian-hackers.

Frederiksen, C. H. (2018) The role of Denmark in a more complex security environment. *Danish Foreign Policy Yearbook, 32-43.* Copenhagen

Fruhlinger, J. (2020, February 12) The OPM hack explained: Bad security practices meet China's Captain America. CSO Online, International Data Group (IDG) Communication, Inc. https://www.csoonline.com/article/3318238/the-opm-hack-explained-bad-security-practices-meet-chinas-captain-america.html.

Galexia (2015), EU cybersecurity dashboard, a path to a secure European Cyberspace. www.bsa.org.

Garamone, J. and Ferdinando, L. (2017) DoD Initiates Process to Elevate U.S. Cyber Command to Unified Combatant Command. Department of Defense (DoD) News.

Ghafur, S., Kristensen, S., Honeyford, K. et al. (2019) A retrospective impact analysis of the WannaCry cyberattack on the NHS. npj *Digit. Med.* 2, 98. https://doi.org/10.1038/s41746-019-0161-6 .

Goldsmith, J. (2011) *Cybersecurity Treaties: A Skeptical View.* Hoover Institution, Stanford University.

Goldsmith, J., and T. Wu (2006) *Who Controls the Internet? Illusions of a Borderless World.* Oxford University Press.

Greiman, V.A. (2015) Cybersecurity and Global Governance. *Journal of Information Warfare* (JIW) 14 (4) 1-14. https://www.jinfowar.com/.

Greiman, V.A. (2019) The Winds of Change in World Politics and the Impact on Cyber Stability. *International Journal of Cyber Warfare and Terrorism* (IJCWT) vol. 9(4) 27-43. DOI: 10.4018/IJCWT.2019100102.

Greiman, V.A. (2021) The Politics and Practice of Cyber Attribution: A Global Legal Perspective. Published in the Proceedings of the International Conference on Cyberwarfare and Security.

Grierson J., Devlin H., (2020, May 3) Hostile states trying to steal coronavirus research. The Guardian. https://www.theguardian.com/world/2020/may/03/hostilestates-trying-to-steal-coronavirus-research-says-uk-agency.

Gries, T. (2020) Germany. Federal Office for Information Security *(Bundesamt für Sicherheit in der Informationstechnik* – BSI).

Gruber, T.R. (1995) Toward principles for the design of ontologies used for knowledge sharing. Presented at the Padua workshop on Formal Ontology, March 1993, later published in *International Journal of Human-Computer Studies*, vol. 43, Issues 4-5, pp. 907-928.

Haimes, V. Y. (2009) On the Definition of Resilience in Systems. *Risk Analysis,* Vol. 29 (4).

Harrop, W. and Matteson, A. (2013) Cyber resilience: A review of critical national infrastructure and cyber security protection measures applied in the UK and USA. *Journal of Business Continuity and Emergency Planning*, vol. 7 (1), 16.

Healey, J., Mosser, P., Rosen, K. and Tache, A. (2018) The future of financial stability and cyber risk. Cyber Security Project at Brookings, Brookings Institution.

HIPPA Journal (2021, January 19) 2020 Healthcare Data Breach Report: 25% Increase in Breaches in 2020.

Hollis, D. (2011) Cyberwar Case Study: Georgia 2008, *Small Wars Journal.* Small Wars Foundation.

Homeland Defense and Global Security (HDGS, 2015) *Space Domain Mission Assurance: A Resilience Taxonomy.* Office of the Assistant Secretary of Defense for Homeland Defense and Global Security, U.S. Department of Defense.

Hopkins A. (2014) Issues in safety science. *Safety Sci.* vol. 67, 6-14.

Housen-Couriel, D. (2017) National Cyber Security Organization Israel. NATO Cooperative Cyber Defense Center of Excellence (CCD COE), Tallinn, Estonia,

Howard, J. D. (1997) An Analysis of Security Incidents on the Internet 1989-1995. Doctoral dissertation, Carnegie Mellon University, Pittsburgh, PA.

Hughes O. (2018) Norway healthcare cyber-attack could be biggest of its kind. *Digital Health.* https://www.digitalhealth.net/2018/01/norway-healthcare-cyber-attack-could-be-biggest/.

Idaho National Laboratory (INL) (2016, August) Cyber Threat and Vulnerability Analysis of the U.S. Electric Sector, Mission Support Center Analysis Report, Mission Support Center.

Intelligence National Security Alliance. (INSA) (2013) Operational Levels of Cyber Intelligence, Intelligence and National Security Alliance, Cyber Intelligence Task Force White Paper, September.

Intelligence National Security Alliance. (INSA) (2014) Strategic Cyber Intelligence. Intelligence and National Security Alliance, Cyber Intelligence Task Force White Paper, March.

International Law Commission (2021) https://legal.un.org/ilc/.

International Organization of Securities Commissions (OICU-IOSCO) (2020) *Principles on Outsourcing.* Consultation Report, May. The Board of the International Organization of Securities Commissions. https://www.iosco.org/library/pubdocs/pdf/IOSCOPD654.pdf.

International Telecommunications Union (ITU) (2015) *Global Cybersecurity Agenda.* General Secretariat, Geneva.

International Telecommunication Union (ITU) (2020) *Measuring digital development: Facts and figures.* Geneva. https://www.itu.int/en/ITU-D/Statistics/Pages/facts/default.aspx.

IRGC (2020), Involving stakeholders in the risk governance process. EPFL, International Risk Governance Center, Lausanne.

Irwin, L. (2018, February 1) Breach at Norway's largest healthcare authority was a disaster waiting to happen., February 1, IT Governance European Blog. https://www.itgovernance.eu/blog/en/breach-at-norways-largest-healthcare-authority-was-a-disaster-waiting-to-happen.

Israel National Cyber Directorate (2020) https://www.gov.il/en/departments/israel_national_cyber_directorate.

Jalali, M.S. and Kaiser, J.P. (2018) Cybersecurity at Hospitals: A Systematic, Organizational Perspective. *J. Med Internet Res.* vol. 20 (5): e10059. doi: 10.2196/10059.

Japan. (2015) *Japan Cybersecurity Strategy.* The Government of Japan.

Joshi, C. and Singh, U.K. (2014) ADMIT: A Five-Dimensional Approach Towards Standardization of Network and Computer Attack Taxonomies. *International Journal of Computer Application* vol. 100 (5), 30-36.

Joshi, C., and Singh, U.K. (2015) A Review on Taxonomies of Attacks and Vulnerability in Computer and Network System. *International Journal of Advanced Research in Computer Science and Software Engineering,* vol. 5 (1), January.

Joubert, V. and Samaan, J-L. (2014) L'intergouvernementalité dans le cyberespace : étude comparée des initiatives de l'Otan et de l'UE, Hérodote 2014/1-2 (n° 152-153), 261 – 275.

Khandelwal S. (2018) Nearly half of the Norway population exposed in HealthCare data breach. The Hacker News 2018. https://thehackernews.com/2018/01/healthcare-data-breach.html.

References

Khare, S. (2020, November 11). Cybercriminals target the pharmaceutical industry. https://www.whitehatsec.com/blog/cybercriminals-target-the-pharmaceutical-industry/.

Kikuchi, M. and Okubo, T. (2020) Building Cyber Resilience through Polycentric Governance. *Journal of Communication*, vol. 15 (5).

Killourhy, K. S., Maxion, R. A., & Tan, K. M. C. (2004) A Defense-Centric Taxonomy Based on Attack Manifestation. Presented at the International Conference on Dependable Systems & Networks, Florence, Italy.

Kitten, T., and Schwartz, M. (2016, April 25) Bangladesh Bank Heist: Lessons Learned Malware Attack Highlights Need for Better Network Intrusion Detection. Bank Info Security.

Klimburg, A. (ed.) (2012) *NATO Cyber Security Framework Manual.* NATO Cooperative Cyber Defense Center of Excellence (CCD COE), Tallinn, Estonia, December.

Koening, D.R. (2015) *Governance Reimagined: Organizational Design, Risk and Value Creation.* John Wiley & Sons, Hoboken.

Koh, H. H. (2012, September 18) International Law in Cyberspace: Remarks as Prepared for Delivery to the USCYBERCOM Inter-Agency Legal Conference reprinted in 54 *Harvard International Law Journal* Online, 2012, December 3.

Kohler, K. (2020, September) *Estonia's National Cybersecurity and Cyberdefense Posture.* Cyberdefense Report Policy and Organizations. Cyber Defense Project, Center for Security Studies (CSS), ETH Zürich. DOI: 10.3929/ethz-b-000438276

KPMG (2015) Health Care and Cyber Security: Increasing Threats Require Increased Capabilities. https://assets.kpmg/content/dam/kpmg/pdf/2015/09/cyber-health-care-survey-kpmg-2015.pdf.

KPMG. (2017) Overview of China's cybersecurity law.

Kruger, L. G. (2016, November 18) *Internet Governance and the Domain Name System: Issues for Congress.* Congressional Research Service. https://fas.org/sgp/crs/misc/R42351.pdf.

LabMD, Inc. v. FTC, No. 16-16270 (11th Cir. June 6, 2018).

LabMD, Inc., (F.T.C. Aug. 29, 2013) (No. 9357), 2013 WL 4761163.

Latici, T. (2020) Understanding the EU's approach to cyber diplomacy and cyber defence, European Parliamentary Research Service.

Latour, B. (2005) *Reassembling the social. An introduction to Actor-Network Theory.* Oxford University Press, Oxford.

Levite, A. and Jinghua, L (2019, January 24) *Chinese American Relations in Cyberspace: Toward Collaboration or Confrontation.* Carnegie Endowment for International Peace.

Linkov, I., Eisenberg, D. A., Plourde, K., Seager, T. P., Allen, J., & Kott, A. (2013). Resilience metrics for cyber systems. *Environment Systems and Decisions: Formerly the Environmentalist*, vol. 33 (4), 471.

Linkov, I., and Trump, B.D. (2019) *The Science and Practice of Resilience*, Springer.

Linkov, I., Trump, B.D., Hynes, W. (2019) *Resilience Strategies and Approaches to Contain Systemic Threats.* General Secretariat, OECD.

Linnaeus, Carl (1735) *Systema Naturae Linnaeus*, Carl (1758). *Systema naturae per regna tria naturae: secundum classes, ordines, genera, species, cum characteribus, differentiis, synonymis, locis* (in Latin) (10th ed.). Laurentius Salvius, Stockholm.

Lithuania (2018) *National Cyber Security Strategy.* Resolution No. 818 of the Government of the Republic of Lithuania.

Lloyd's Emerging Risks Report (2017). *Counting the cost: Cyber exposure decoded.* Lloyd's and Cyence, London.

Manto, C.L. and Lokmer, S. (eds.) (2015) *Planning Resilience for High-Impact Threats to Critical Infrastructure,* p. 199, Infraguard, Westphalia, Press.

Matishak, M. (2017, August 18). Trump elevates U.S. Cyber Command, vows 'increased re-solve' against threats, Politico.

Maurer, T. and Nelson, A. (2020) *International Strategy to Better Protect the Financial System Against Cyber Threats.* Carnegie Endowment for International Peace in collaboration with World Economic Forum.

McGinnis, M. D. (2016) Polycentric Governance in Theory and Practice: Dimensions of Aspiration and Practical Limitations. SSRN: https://ssrn.com/abstract=3812455 or http://dx.doi.org/10.2139/ssrn.3812455.

Medelyan, O., Witten, I.H., Divolie, A. Broekstra, J., (2013) *Automatic construction of lexicons, taxonomies, ontologies, and other knowledge structures.* Wiley, Hoboken, New York.

Microsoft Blog. (2020, December 17) Brad Smith, President. A moment of reckoning: The need for a strong and global cyber security response. https://blogs.microsoft.com/on-the-issues/2020/12/17/cyberattacks-cybersecurity-solarwinds-fireeye/.

Microsoft Cyber Defense Operations Center: Strategy Brief. (2017)

Millard, W. B. (2017) Where bits and bytes meet flesh and blood. *Annals of Emerg Med.* vol. 70 (3), September. https://www.annemergmed.com/article/S0196-0644(17)30891-0/pdf..

MITRE (2015) Addressing Cyber Resiliency in a Conventional Cyber Security Focused World, MITRE Fifth Annual Secure and Resilient Cyber Architectures Invitational.

Morris, D.Z. and Hackett, R. (2021, January 29) After Solar Winds: Untangling America's Cyber Security Mess. Fortune, New York, NY.

Muthuppalaniappan, M. and Stevenson, K. (2021) Healthcare cyber-attacks and the COVID-19 pandemic: an urgent threat to global health. *International Journal for Quality in Health Care,* vol. 33 (1), mzaa117, https://doi.org/10.1093/intqhc/mzaa117.

National Academy of Sciences, Engineering and Medicine. (NAS) (2012) *Disaster Resilience: A National Imperative.* National Academies Press (2012).

National Institute of Standards and Technology (NIST) (2018) *Framework for Improving Critical Infrastructure Cybersecurity Version 1.1.* U.S. Department of Commerce. Washington, D.C. NIST/FSB Cyber Lexicon. https://nvl-pubs.nist.gov/nistpubs/CSWP/NIST.CSWP.04162018.pdf.

National Public Radio (NPR) (2015, June 13) Ex-NSA Officer: OPM Hack Is Serious Breach of Worker Trust. https://www.npr.org/2015/06/13/414149626/ex-nsa-officer-opm-hack-is-serious-breach-of-worker-trust.

National Security Agency (NSA) (2017).) *Joint Statement for the Record to the Senate Armed Services Committee, Foreign Cyber Threats to the United States.* The Honorable James Clapper, Director of National Intelligence, The Honorable Marcel Lettre, Undersecretary of Defense for Intelligence, Admiral Michael S. Rogers, USN Commander, U.S. Cyber Command Director, National Security Agency (NSA), Washington, D.C., January 5.

NATO Cooperative Cyber Defence Centre of Excellence (CCD COE) (2017) *The Tallinn Manual 2.0 on the International Law Applicable to Cyber Operations*, (Michael Schmitt and Liis Vihul (eds.)) Cambridge University Press, Cambridge, England.

Netherlands (2018) *National Cyber Security Agenda.* Ministry of Justice and Security, The Netherlands.

Newman, L.M. (2020, September 28) A Ransomware Attack Has Struck a Major US Hospital Chain, Wired. https://www.wired.com/story/universal-health-services-ransomware-attack/.

Nicholas, P. and Pinter, J. (2017) *Cyber Resilience Digitally Empowering Cities.* Microsoft. https://query.prod.cms.rt.microsoft.com/cms/api/am/binary/RW6auc

North Atlantic Treaty Organization (NATO) (2020) *Cyber Defense.* https://www.nato.int/cps/en/natohq/topics_78170.htm.

References

Norway National Cyber Security Strategy (2019) Norwegian Ministries. https://www.regjeringen.no/contentassets/c57a0733652f47688294934ffd93fc53/national-cyber-security-strategy-for-norway.pdf.

Nye, J. S. (2010) *Cyber Power*. The Belfer Center, Kennedy School of Government/

Oregon Department of Justice (2019, July 22) 50 State Attorneys General Secure $600 Million from Equifax in Largest Data Breach Settlement in History.https://www.doj.state.or.us/media-home/news-media-releases/50-state-attorneys-general-secure-600-million-from-equifax-in-largest-data-breach-settlement-in-history/.

Organization for Economic Cooperation and Development (OECD) (2017) *Key Issues for Digital Transformation in the G20.* Report prepared for a joint G20 German Presidency/OECD Conference, Berlin, Germany, 12 January. The Secretary General, OECD Directorate for Science, Technology and Innovation, Paris.

Organization for Economic Cooperation and Development. (OECD) (2019) *Resilience Strategies and Approaches to Contain Systemic Threats,* 17-18 September, General Secretariat.

Paris Call for Trust and Security in Cyberspace (Paris) (2018, November) Presented at the Internet Governance Forum held at UNESCO and the Paris Peace Forum.

Pearlson, K.E., Saunders, C.S. and Galleta, D. F. (2016) *Managing and Using Information Systems: A Strategic Approach,* 6th ed. John Wiley & Sons, Hoboken.

Periroth, N. and Satariano, A. (2021, May 20) Irish Hospitals are latest to be hit by Ransomware Attacks, New York Times.

Ponemon Institute. (2008) Airport Insecurity: The Case of Missing and Lost Laptops. Executive Summary, U.S. Research. https://www.dell.com/downloads/global/services/dell_lost_laptop_study.pdf.

Ponemon Institute, (2017) Etude annuelle sur la cyber-résilience : Focus sur les résultats en France.

Ponemon Institute IBM Security (Ponemon) (2018) *Cost of a Data Breach Report 2018: Impact of Business Continuity Management.*

Ponemon Institute IBM Security (Ponemon) (2019) *Cost of a Data Breach Report 2019.*

Ponemon Institute IBM Security (Ponemon) (2020) *Cost of a Data Breach Report 2020.*

Quatris Health. (2016) Centricity Down After Applying Windows Updates. http://www.quatris.com/messagecenter/centricity-services-update-centricity-applying-windows-updates/.

Republic of Turkey (2020) *National Cybersecurity Strategy and Action Plan (2020-2023)* Presidency of the Republic of Turkey Ministry of Transport and Infrastructure., December 29, Rid, T. (2013) *Cyber War Will Not Take Place.* Oxford University Press, Oxford.

Röhrig,W. & Smeaton R. (2015) *Cyber Security and Cyber Defence in The European Union.* https://www.cybersecurity-review.com/articles/cyber-security-and-cyber-defence-in-the-european-union/

Ross, R., Pillitteri, V. Graubart, R., Bodeau, D., McQuaid, R. (2019) *Developing Cyber Resilient Systems: A Systems Security Engineering Approach.* NIST Special Publication Vol. 2, 800-160.

Russia Yarovaya Law. 374-FZ and 375-FZ, June 22, 2016.

Rustad, M. (2020) *Global Internet Law*. 3rd ed. St. Paul, Minn: West Academic Publishing.

Samonek, A. (2020). What Is the Future of European Cyber Security? Three Principles of European Cooperation and the Hybrid Joint Strategy of Cyber Defence. *Studia Europejskie*, *24*(2), 43–60.

Sanchez, G. (2015) Case Study: Critical Controls that Sony Should Have Implemented, Sans Institute.

Santamaria, M. (2016) 45% of Healthcare Breaches Occur on Stolen Laptops, https://www.digicert.com/dc/blog/45-percent-healthcare-breaches-occur-on-laptops/.

Saudi Arabia Cyber World Summit (2020, November 3). Saudi Arabia's tech leaders unite to push for a more Cyber-Resilient future for the region.

Schallbruch, M. amd Skierka, I. M. (2018). The Organisation of Cybersecurity in Germany. July. DOI: 10.1007/978-3-319-90014-8, ESMT European School of Management and Technology.

Schwartz, M. (2014, December 23) Sony's 7 Breach Response Mistakes - BankInfoSecurity. https://www.bankinfosecurity.com/sony-breach-response-legal-threats-a-7676.

Schwartz, M. (2020, July 30) Questions Persist about Ransomware Attack on Blackbaud. https://www.bankinfosecurity.com/ransomware-attack-questions-persist-over-black-baud-hit-a-14734.

Scott D. and Angelos, S. (2013) Towards a Cyber Conflict Taxonomy", 5th International Conference on Cyber Conflict. K. Pod ins, J. Stinissen, M. Maybaum.

Senate (2017, January 5) Foreign cyber threats to the United States. Hearing Before the Committee on Armed Services. United States Senate One Hundred Fifteenth Congress First Session.

Senate (2019, March 6) How Equifax neglected cybersecurity and suffered a devastating data breach. U.S. Senate, Permanent Subcommittee on investigations, Committee on Homeland Security and Governmental Affairs.

Shackelford, S. J., Russell, S. Haut, J. (2016). Bottoms Up: A Comparison of 'Voluntary' Cybersecurity Frameworks.16 U.C. Davis. *Bus. Law Journal*, 217, spring.

Shapiro, J. (1994) Digital Object Identifier, *IEEE Spectrum*, vol. 31 (6) 56 – 59.

Shea, J. (2017) Resilience: a core element of collective defence. NATO Review magazine.

Simmons, C., Ellis, C., Shiva, S., Dasgupta, D., Wu, Q. (2009, January) *Avoidit.* A Cyber-attack Taxonomy, White Paper, University of Memphis, Department of Computer Science. https://www.researchgate.net/publica-tion/229020163_AVOIDIT_A_Cyber_Attack_Taxonomy.

Singapore (2020, April) *Ensuring Safe Management and Operational Resilience of the Financial Sector.* The Monetary Authority of Singapore, https://www.mas.gov.sg/regulation/covid-19/ensuring-safe-distancing-and-operational-resilience-of-the-financial-sector.

Sittig, D. F. and Singh, H. (2016) A socio-technical approach to preventing, mitigating, and recovering from ransomware attacks. *Appl. Clin. Inf.* vol. 7, 624–632.

Slovak Republic (2015) *Cyber Security Concept (2015-2020).* nisa.europa.eu/topics/national-cyber-security-strategies/ncss-map/cyber-security-concept-of-the-slovak-republic-1.

Sobel, N. (2019, September 27) Recent Decision: D.C. Circuit Rules That OPM Breach Victims Have Standing to Sue, Lawfare.

Socta (2017) Serious and Organized Crime Threat Assessment – Crime in the age of technology. European Police Office.

Solum, L. B. (2008) Models of Internet Governance. Illinois Public Law Research Paper No. 07-25, U. Illinois Law & Economics Research Paper No. LE08-027, September 3.

Solutions. (2017) Alliance for Telecommunications Industry, ATIS Telecom Glossary. http://www.atis.org/glossary/annex.aspx.

Spinoza, B. (1985) *The Collected Works of Spinoza*, translated and edited by Edwin Curley, vol. 1, Princeton University Press, Princeton.

Statista. https://www.statista.com/(2015) (2021).

Stine, K., Quinn, S. Witte, G., Gardner, R.K. (2020) *Integrating Cybersecurity and Enterprise Risk Management (ERM).* National Institute of Standards and Technology, U.S. Department of Commerce. Nistir 8286.

Tanev G, Apiafi R. (2015) A Value Blueprint Approach to Cybersecurity in Networked Medical Devices. *Technol Innov Manag Rev.* vol. 5(6), 17–25. 10.22215/timreview/903.

References

Thinyane, M. and Christine, D. (2020) *Cyber Resilience in Asia-Pacific-A Review of National Cybersecurity Strategies*, United Nations University, Institute in Macau.

Tsai, J. (2008) *Machine Learning in Cyber Trust: Security, Privacy and Reliability*, Springer.

United Kingdom (UK) *Cyber Security Strategy 2016-2021*. (2020). Progress Report Autumn 2020. Cabinet Office.

United Kingdom Financial Conduct Authority (UK FCA) (2018, October 1) Final Notice Tesco Personal Finance plc.

UN Department of Economic and Social Affairs (UNDESA) (2020) eGovernment Report.

UNISDR. (2015) *Global Assessment Report on Disaster Reports on Disaster Risk Reduction (GAR)*, Risk Reduction Making Development Sustainable: the future of disaster risk management. UNISDR, Geneva, Switzerland.

UNISDR. (2016) *UNISDR Strategic Framework 2016-2021 in Support of the Sendai Framework for Disaster Risk Reduction 2015-2030*. UNISDR, Office for Disaster Risk Reduction, Geneva, Switzerland.

United States Cyberspace Solarium Commission (CSC) (2020) *Cyberspace Solarium Commission Report*. Washington, D.C.
 https://drive.google.com/file/d/1ryMCIL_dZ30QyjFqFkkf10MxIXJGT4yv/view.

United States Department of Health and Human Services (HHS) (2017) *Information Technology Strategic Plan, FY 2017-2020*. HHS, Washington, D.C.

United States Department of Health and Human Services (HHS) (2021, January 15) Health Insurer Pays $5.1 Million to Settle Data Breach Affecting Over 9.3 million People. HHS, Washington, D.C. https://www.hhs.gov/about/news/2021/01/15/health-insurer-pays-5-1-million-settle-data-breach.html.

United States Department of Treasury (2019, September 13). Treasury Sanctions North Korean State-Sponsored Malicious Cyber Groups. https://home.treasury.gov/news/press-releases/sm774.

United States Department of Treasury (2020, October 1) Ransomware Advisory. Office of the Foreign Assets Control. https://home.treasury.gov/policy-issues/financial-sanctions/recent-actions/20201001.

United States House of Representatives (HR) (2016) Committee on Oversight and Government Reform. *The OPM Data Breach: How the Government Jeopardized Our National Security for More than a Generation*. Majority Staff Report, 114th Congress. September 7, 2016. https://republicans-oversight.house.gov/wp-content/uploads/2016/09/The-OPM-Data-Breach-How-the-Government-Jeopardized-Our-National-Security-for-More-than-a-Generation.pdf

United States House of Representatives (HR) (2018) Committee on Oversight and Government Reform. *The Equifax Data Breach Majority Staff Report* 115th Congress December 2018.

United States House of Representatives (HR) (2021) National Defense Authorization Act for Fiscal Year 2021. 116th Congress (2019-2020).

Vaughan, D. (2016) *The Challenger Launch Decision: Risky Technology, Culture, and Deviance at NASA,* University of Chicago Press. pp. 30–1. ISBN 978-0-226-34696-0.

VentureBeat. (2011, September 22) Security lessons from the PlayStation Network breach | VentureBeat | News | by VentureBeat. http://venturebeat.com/2011/09/22/security-lessons-from-the-playstationnetwork-breach/

Verhulst, S.G., B. S. Noveck, J. Raines and A. Declercq. (2014) Innovations in Global Governance: Toward a Distributed Internet Governance Ecosystem, Paper Series: No. 5, December, Global Commission on Internet Governance, Chatham House, London.

Vogus TJ, Sutcliffe KM. (2012) Organizational mindfulness and mindful organizing: a reconciliation and path forward. *Acad Man Learn Ed*. vol. 11, 722-735.

Waldrop, M. (2015) DARPA and the Internet Revolution. The Defense Advanced Research Projects Agency (DARPA), U.S. Department of Defense, Washington, D.C.

Warwick A. (2018) Norwegian healthcare breach alert failed GDPR requirements. Computer Weekly. http://www.computerweekly.com/news/252433538/Norwegian-healthcare-breach-alert-failed-GDPR-requirements.

Waters, D. (2011) *Supply Chain Risk Management* (2nd ed.). Kogan Page, London.

Weick KE, Sutcliffe KM. (2015) *Managing the Unexpected: Sustained Performance in a Complex World.* (3rd ed.) John Wiley & Sons, Hoboken.

White House (WH) (2011) *International Strategy for Cyber Space: Prosperity, Security and Openness in a Networked World.* Executive Office of the President, Washington, DC.

White House (WH) (2012) Presidential Policy Directive (PPD-20) U.S. Cyber Operations Policy, Executive Office of the President, Washington, DC.

White House (WH) (2013) Presidential Policy Directive (PPD-21) Critical Infrastructure Security and Resilience, The White House Office of the Press Secretary, February 12.

White House (WH) (2016a) Presidential Policy Directive (PPD- 41), July 26. United States Cyber Incident Coordination, Executive Office of the President, Washington, DC.

White House (WH) (2016b) Commission on Enhancing National Cybersecurity. *Report on Securing and Growing the Digital Economy.* Executive Order 13718, Executive Office of the President, Washington, DC.

White House (WH) (2017) Office of the Press Secretary, Presidential Executive Order 13800 on Strengthening the Cybersecurity of Federal Networks and Critical Infrastructure. May 11.

White House Executive Office (WH) (NSTC) (2020) *Recommendations for Strengthening American Leadership in Industries of the Future.* A Report to the President of the United States of America, The President's Council of Advisors on Science and Technology. https://science.osti.gov/-/media/_/pdf/about/pcast/202006/PCAST_June_2020_Report.pdf?la=en&hash=019A4F17C79FDEE5005C51D3D6CAC81FB31E3ABC.

White House (WH) (2021) Executive Order on Improving the Nation's Cybersecurity, May 12, The Executive Office of the President.

Wiley (2015) Lessons to be Learned from the Sony Breach. Wiley Newsletter. https://www.wiley.law/newsletter-5211.

World Bank (2019, July 18) Financial Inclusion Global Initiative (FIGI) https://www.worldbank.org/en/topic/financialinclusion/brief/figi.

World Economic Forum (WEF) (2016). *A Framework for Assessing Cyber Resilience: A Report for the World Economic Forum*, April 28.

World Health Organization (WHO) (2019) *Global Spending on Health: A World in Transition, Global Report 2019,* WHO, Switzerland.

The World Summit on the Information Society (WSIS) (2005). *Tunis Agenda for the Information Society*, para 34. [Geneva 2003 – Tunis 2005] WSIS-05/TUNIS/DOC/6(Rev.1) E. November 18.

Yeli, H. (2017) Unity of Opposites in Cyber Sovereignty as per Three-Perspectives Theory, in an occasional paper. China Institute for international Strategic Studies.

Zetter, Kim (2016a, March 3) Inside the Cunning, Unprecedented Attack. https://www.wired.com/2016/03/inside-cunning-unprecedented-hack-ukraines-power-grid/precedented Hack of Ukraine's Power Grid, Wired.

Zetter, Kim (2016b, May 17) That Insane, $81M Bangladesh Bank Heist? Here's What We Know. Wired. https://www.wired.com/2016/05/insane-81m-bangladesh-bank-heist-heres-know

Index

Printed in the USA
CPSIA information can be obtained
at www.ICGtesting.com
LVHW061448150823
755320LV00011B/649